Ketogenic Instant Pot Cookbook

The best 100 Keto Instant Pot Recipes To Lose Weight and Being Healthy!

Virginia Hoffman

Introduction

I want to thank you and congratulate you for buying the book, *"Ketogenic Instant Pot Cookbook"*.

This book has 100+ delicious instant pot recipes that you can prepare while on the Ketogenic diet.

The Ketogenic diet is without doubt a must follow diet if you want to lose weight, keep it off and obtain various other benefits such as making your skin healthy, fighting cancer, restoring insulin sensitivity and much, much more. Whether you've just started following the diet or have already been following the diet with impressive results, you must perhaps have noticed that one of the challenging parts about following the diet is preparing delicious meals especially when you have a busy schedule.

If you still want to stay committed to the diet, one thing you want to prioritize is cooking foods fast while of course ensuring you retain the nutrients. There is no better way to achieve that than use a pressure cooker and in particular, the modern, technologically advanced pressure cooker, known as instant pot.

Think about it, with the instant pot, it does more than just cook; it can switch itself off when food is cooked, can sauté, steam, can act as a rice cooker, yogurt maker, can fry and do just about everything that all your other kitchen appliances can do, all in one! That's not all; the instant pot comes with a delay start function, a feature which allows you to add ingredients to the instant pot then set the cooker to start cooking at a specific time, which essentially means you can wake up to a hot breakfast or come home to a hot dinner!

What this means is that if you are following a Ketogenic diet, you have no reason not to easily and quickly prepare meals at home. If you excited to start using the instant pot to make it easier for you to follow the Ketogenic diet, this book, has 100+ delicious Ketogenic diet friendly recipes that you can prepare using an instant pot. What makes the book even handy is the fact that the recipes are classified into categories that you will be excited about i.e. chicken, meat, veggies, seafood, soup etc. Let's begin.

Thanks again for downloading this book. I hope you enjoy it!

Note: To see the pic of the recipes, please refer to the kindle version of this book

Table of Contents

Although this book is primarily a cookbook, I strongly believe it would be great if we started by briefly touching on some basics for the benefit of complete beginners. So if you are not a beginner to the Ketogenic diet, you are free to skip this part.

Note: To see the pic of the recipes, please refer to the kindle version of this book

Chapter1: Ketogenic Diet: A Beginner Friendly Background

What is Ketogenic Diet?

The term Ketogenic is derived from 2 terms namely "Keto", which means "ketone" and "Genic" which means to produce. This means it is a ketone producing diet i.e. without the production of ketones, you cannot be said to be in a Ketogenic diet. The purpose of the diet is to make the body to enter into a nutritional state referred to as ketosis i.e. a state where the body produces and burns ketones (a product of the metabolism of fats) for energy.

For the body to produce ketones, you have to reduce your carbohydrates intake significantly, take lots of fats and take a moderate amount of proteins. When this happens, you start reversing everything that the body has been doing regarding fat storage. More precisely, with reduced carb intake, the immediate effect is a reduction in the blood glucose levels, which is followed by a reduction in the amounts of insulin that the body produces. Instead, the body produces more of glucagon, a hormone that triggers the liver to start metabolizing stored glycogen from the liver and muscle cells.

At the same time, the body produces the human growth hormone, which along with glucagon triggers the release of fats from fat stores around the body after which these fats are transported to the liver. The liver then breaks the fats (they are usually in the form of triglycerides) into fatty acids and glycerol. The fatty acids then go through a series of processes that ultimately produce ketone bodies, which the body uses as fuel, just like glucose. As the body converts more of fats to fatty acids and glycerol and subsequently ketone bodies, this increases the body's reliance on ketones, which slowly increases to a point where a significant part of the body processes are running on ketones. This is referred to as nutritional/optimal ketosis and sets in when the level of ketone concentration in the bloodstream is 1.5 – 3 mmol/L.

For this to happen, you have to limit your carb intake to between 20grams and 50 grams daily, take about 0.7-1gram of protein for every pound of body weight and take as much fat as you want (the fat should account for about 65-75% of daily calories taken).

With that in mind, I know you might be wondering; why should you take lots of fats and why should you take moderate amount of proteins? Let me answer that:

Why should you take lots of fats?

The reason why you have to take lots of fats is to give your body enough energy without having to increase your carbohydrate consumption. This is especially great since fats don't trigger the production of insulin (insulin hinders fat metabolism). Also, fats tend to be filling, slow to digest and help keep cravings at bay, a phenomenon that can greatly help in the process of weight loss.

Why should your protein intake be moderate?

The reason why you take a moderate amount of proteins is to avoid chances of the body converting any excess protein into carbohydrates in a process referred to as gluconeogenesis; you need just enough for muscle repair and maintenance.

So which carbs, proteins and fats should you take in order to get into ketosis? Let's discuss that next.

Eating Keto

- Which Foods Should You Eat?

1. Veggies

Vegetables, especially the leafy green veggies, are a good source of vitamins, which helps enhance your immune system's ability to fight diseases.

Note: The veggies allowed in Keto diet should be high in nutrients and low in carbohydrates. Therefore, you should strictly avoid starchy carbs. Eat a wide variety of green vegetables such as kales, cucumber, broccoli, asparagus, collard greens and mushrooms. Also, try the following veggies among others:

- Red/Green bell pepper
- Onion
- Tomatoes
- Yellow squash
- Flat-leaf parsley
- Button mushrooms
- Spinach
- Head leaf lettuce
- Zucchini
- Jalapeno pepper
- Cauliflower

- Eggplant
- Parsley flakes
- Carrots
- Radishes

2. Proteins

This food group forms a considerable part of the Ketogenic diet plan, as it facilitates general growth as well as repair of worn out cells. Proteins also help in the synthesis and monitoring of hormones that control various bodily functions. Eat fish like catfish, salmon, trout, tuna, mackerel and cod fish. You can also eat white and red meat from animals chicken, ducks, turkey, pork, goats, lamb and cattle.

Here are examples of meats, fish, poultry and other protein foods that you can consume:

- Bacon
- Eggs
- Chorizo
- Chicken breasts/sticks
- Lobster
- Chicken stock
- Haddock
- Scallops
- Deveined shrimp
- Ham
- Pork sausage rinds
- Ground turkey
- Hot Italian sausage

- Ducks breast
- Turkey pepperoni
- Lean deli ham
- Canned tuna

3. Fats and Oils

The most recommended fats to consume are omega 3 fatty oils, which include fish like salmon, tuna and trout just to mention a few. Additionally, you should take saturated and mono saturated fats like butter, macadamia nuts, avocados, egg yolks and coconut oils. These fats are preferred because they have a stable chemical structure, which is less inflammatory. As a beginner in Keto diet, here a few examples of fats, oils and dairy allowed in the diet:

- Mozzarella cheese
- Olive oil
- Butter
- Cheddar cheese
- Heavy whipping cream
- Sour cream
- Vegetable oil
- Parmesan cheese
- Organic coconut oil
- Cottage cheese

4. Nuts, Seeds and Fruits

You can also eat moderate amounts of low-carb fruits, nuts and seeds to help control carb intake. Here's what to put on your plate:

- Pecans
- Celery seed
- Sesame seeds
- Tahini
- Walnuts
- Almond flour
- Flax seed meal
- Raisins
- Sunflower seeds

Fruits

Most fruits are rich in sugars, fructose and carbs and thus you only eat only a few types of them, and in moderation. You can enjoy various fruits such as:

- Blueberries
- Avocado
- Cranberries
- Olives
- Strawberries
- Blackberries
- Coconut
- Rhubarb
- Raspberries

5. Beverages/drinks

There are a few drinks you can enjoy but ensure that the drinks you take are plain or unsweetened to monitor carb intake.

- Water
- Herbal tea
- Lemon and lime juice

- Soy milk
- Almond milk
- Clear broth, bone broth
- Decaf tea
- Flavored seltzer water
- Coconut milk
- Decaf coffee

Foods To Avoid

1. Sugars

Snacks such as chips, pastries, cookies, pretzels and wheat thin are your number one enemy since they are processed and contain added sugars. The rule of the thumb is to avoid majority of sweet products, or any food substance that contains sugar, honey or sucrose. The following are the culprits in terms of high sugar content:

- Brown sugar

- Fruit juices, fruit syrup and concentrates

- Canned soups and stews

- Rice and maple syrup

- Fructose

- Maltose, barley malt and malt powder

- Coconut sugar

- Brown rice syrup

- Cane sugar, syrup and cane juice

- Agave nectar and honey

2. Grains And Related Products

These too are forms of sugars, are high in carbs and more likely to cause sugar-crashes and weight gain. Avoid all grains and their products such as:

- Pretzels
- Cakes, pies
- Cookies, tarts
- Crackers
- Tortillas
- Cold cereals, hot cereals
- Wheat-based pasta
- Waffles, pancakes
- Cereals
- English muffins
- Sandwiches
- Wheat Thins
- Oatmeal
- Corn
- High-fructose corn syrup

- Whole wheat Pancakes

Be aware that grain derivatives such as corn chips, cornmeal, popcorn and cornbread can be used as preservatives or thickeners in some foods. Ensure that you read list of ingredients first before you purchase packaged food products.

3. Sugary Beverages

Most energy drinks, beers, fruit juices and non-diet sodas have high sugar content and often disrupt fat metabolism, as they raise the level of insulin. Therefore, avoid high-carb beverages among them:

- Alcohol

- Fruits juices

- Sweet or dessert wines

- Non-diet sodas

- Energy drinks

4. Ordinary Milk

You should avoid cow milk due to presence lactose. Instead, drink yoghurt or other fermented milk products.

Alternatively, you can drink milk or dairy alternatives such as almond milk, coconut milk etc. Kindly refer to the allowed beverages on ketogenic diet.

5. Legumes

Though legumes do contain significant quantity of proteins, you should avoid them due to their high starch content. As Ketogenic is basically a low-carb diet, you shouldn't eat any type of beans, peanuts and lentils.

To make your transition to the Ketogenic diet as smooth as possible, it's important to be prepared for it. With a good plan, it's easy task to strictly consume only Ketogenic diet friendly ingredients of your choice. Lucky for you, this book will make this possible by discussing 75 delicious keto diet recipes that you can prepare with your instant pot to ensure you retain the nutrients and prepare your meals fast.

Note: To see the pic of the recipes, please refer to the kindle version of this book

Chapter 2: Chicken Recipes

1. Pressure Cooker Chicken

Serves: 8

Ingredients

6 cloves garlic, peeled

1/2 teaspoon sea salt

2 tablespoons lemon juice

1/4 teaspoon freshly ground black pepper

1 teaspoon dried thyme

1 1/2 cups organic chicken bone broth

1 teaspoon paprika

1 tablespoon organic virgin coconut oil

1 (4lb.) organic chicken

Directions

1. Mix together thyme, paprika, pepper and salt in a small bowl. Rub the seasoning all over the chicken.

2. Add oil in an instant pot and then press the sauté. Add in the chicken, breast side facing down and cook for about 6 to 7 minutes.

3. Flip the bird and add broth, garlic cloves and lemon juice. Lock the lid in place and cook at manual high pressure for 25 minutes.

4. Once the time elapses, allow the pressure to release naturally then open the lid. Serve and enjoy.

Nutritional Information For Recipe: Calories 4132, Carbs 8.32 g, Fat 302g, Protein 326.84g

2. Italian Chicken

Serves: 6

Ingredients

¾ cup mushrooms, thinly sliced

2 lb. chicken breasts

2 tablespoons pesto

¾ cup marinara

¼ teaspoon salt

½ cup red bell pepper

½ cup green bell pepper

¾ cup onion

1 tablespoon olive oil

Directions

1. Press sauté button on your instant pot then add bell peppers, olive oil, salt and onion into the instant pot.

2. Cook until the veggies are soft, for 3-4 minutes. Then add pesto, chicken and the marinara sauce.

3. Cook thawed chicken for 12 minutes at high pressure then quick release pressure.

4. Transfer the chicken to a cutting board or plate and shred using two forks.

5. Remove at least half of the broth from the pot, but leave behind the veggies. Now add in mushrooms and set to sauté until mushrooms are soft or for 2-3 minutes.

6. After about 2-3 minutes, return the chicken to the cooking pot and mix with other ingredients. Serve.

Nutritional Information Per Serving: Calories 153, Carbs: 6.4g, Fat: 11.2g, Protein: 7.6g

3. Creamy Chicken Bacon Ranch

Serves: 6

Ingredients

Green onions

4 oz. light cream cheese, cubed

2 lbs. chicken breasts

1 oz. packet ranch seasoning

1 cup chicken broth

¼ cup raw bacon, chopped

Directions

1. Press the sauté button then add in the bacon. Cook until the bacon is crisped, for 3-4 minutes.

2. Then add in chicken, ranch seasoning and chicken broth. Cook frozen chicken at high pressure for 20 minutes and 12 minutes at high pressure for thawed chicken.

3. Quick release pressure and then transfer the chicken to a cutting board or plate. Use two forks to shred the chicken.

4. Remove half of the liquid from cooking pot, add cream cheese and sauté for 2-3 minutes to fully melt the cheese.

5. Return the chicken to the cooking pot and mix well with the broth and melted cheese. Top with diced onions.

Nutritional Information Per Serving: Calories 225.6, 1.9g Carbs, 12.7g Fat, 24.2g Protein

4. Low Carb Curry Chicken

Serves 3

Ingredients

1 tablespoon arrowroot powder

1 tablespoon lemon juice

1 tablespoon apple cider vinegar

1/4 teaspoon ground cloves

2 teaspoons ground cumin

2 teaspoons curry powder

2 tablespoons garlic powder

1/2 teaspoon ground ginger

1/2 teaspoon pure liquid stevia

1/2 small yellow onion, diced

3 medium frozen chicken breasts

Directions

1. Add all the ingredients into your instant pot insert and then stir to blend the chicken with the seasonings. You can add a cup of water if needed.

2. Cook the chicken on meat setting for 40 minutes, and then do a quick release. Carefully move the chicken to a plate and shred

3. Add arrowroot powder to the liquid that is left in the cooker to thicken and then whisk continuously to remove any clumps.

4. Return the shredded chicken into the sauce and serve over cauliflower rice.

5. Season with pepper and some salt if you like.

Nutritional Information Per Serving: Calories 153.0, Fat 2.8g, Carbs 8.6g, Protein 18.7g

5. Chicken Puttanesca

Serves: 6

Ingredients

3/4 cup water

1 tablespoon chopped fresh basil

1 tablespoon capers rinsed and drained

6 oz. pitted black olives

14 1/2 oz. canned chopped tomatoes

1/2 teaspoon red chili flakes or to taste

Salt

Black pepper, freshly milled

2 cloves garlic crushed

2 tablespoons extra virgin olive oil

6 chicken thighs skin on

Directions

1. Press the sauté button then heat oil for about a minute. Add in chicken pieces the skin side acing down in batches until browned, in about 5 minutes.

2. Once cooked through, transfer the meat to a plate and then add red chili flakes, chopped basil, capers, garlic, olives, water, chopped tomatoes, salt and pepper to the instant pot.

3. Stir to blend the ingredients then let it simmer for some time. Return the meat to the pot.

4. Turn off the sauté function and then lock the lid. Use the manual setting and adjust it to cook at high pressure for 15 minutes.

5. As soon as the cooking time is up, naturally release pressure for around 12 minutes then quick release any remaining pressure.

6. Serve the dish with vegetables, such as zucchini noodles.

Nutritional Information Per Serving: Calories 343, Carbs: 4g, Fat: 27g, Protein: 19g

6. Jalapeno & Chicken Dip

Serves: 8

Ingredients

½ cup water

½ cup panko bread crumbs

¾ cup sour cream

8 oz. cheddar cheese

3 Jalapenos sliced

8 oz. cream cheese

1 lb. boneless chicken breast

Directions

1. Put the meat, cream cheese, sliced Jalapenos and water in the instant pot.

2. Select manual High pressure for 12 minutes.

3. Do a quick release and then shred the chicken. Stir in sour cream and 6 ounce cheddar cheese.

4. Put in a baking dish and top the mixture with the remaining cheese. Put in the broiler for about 2 to 3 minutes then serve.

Nutritional Information Per Serving: Calories 295.2, Fat 24.8g, Carbs 6.5g, Protein 12.7g

7. Chicken Cacciatore

Serves: 4

Ingredients

1/2 teaspoon dried oregano

1/2 cup diced green bell pepper

1/4 cup diced red bell pepper

1/2 cup diced onion

1/2 (14 ounce) can crushed tomatoes

Olive oil spray

Kosher salt

Fresh pepper to taste

4 chicken thighs, with the bone, skin removed

2 tablespoons chopped parsley or basil

1 bay leaf

Directions

1. Season the meat with salt and pepper then press the sauté function.

2. Lightly coat the cooking pot with oil and then brown the meat for a few minutes on each side. Set the chicken aside.

3. Spray the instant pot with extra oil and add in peppers and onions, sauté for about 5 minutes or until soft and golden.

4. Now pour the tomatoes over the veggies and chicken and then add in salt, pepper, oregano and bay leaf. Stir the mixture and then cover.

5. Cook the ingredients for 25 minutes at high pressure then natural release pressure for a couple of minutes.

Nutritional Information Per Serving: Calories: 133, Fat: 3g, Carbs: 10.5g, Protein 14g

8. Instant pot Chicken Thighs

Serve: 4

Ingredients

1 green onion, sliced

1/2 teaspoon salt

2 tablespoons apple cider vinegar

1 teaspoon fish sauce

1/2 cup chicken broth

2 tablespoons honey

1/4 cup cilantro, chopped

1 1-inch piece of ginger, chopped

1/4 cup + 1 tablespoon coconut aminos, divided

2 tablespoons of lime juice

4 cloves garlic, chopped

1 mango, cut into 1/2 inch chunks

1/2 red onion, chopped

8 chicken thighs, deboned

1 tablespoon cooking fat

Directions

1. Press the sauté button then put cooking fat into the cooking pot. Heat the fat until melted.

2. Put the chicken thighs into the pot, with the skin side facing down. Brown the meat for about 3 minutes.

3. Flip over and brown the other side for 2 minutes. Based on the size of the thighs, you might be required to cook 4 thighs at a time; but, ensure the cooking pot is not overcrowded.

4. Once cooked, remove from the pot and set aside. Then add mango, garlic and onion to the pot. Cook until the mango begins to slightly brown and the onions are clear.

5. Turn off the Instant Pot and put back the chicken into the cooking pot. Nestle into the onion and mango mixture.

6. Now add in lime juice, honey, cilantro, fish sauce, chicken broth, ginger, ¼ cup coconut aminos and a tablespoon of apple cider vinegar.

7. Close the lid, secure it and press the Poultry function. Set it to high pressure and set the timer for 15 minutes. After the Instant Pot goes to Keep Warm mode, turn it off.

8. Then turn pressure valve to venting and make sure pressure is fully released from the pot. Carefully open the lid, and remove the chicken thighs from cooking pot. Set aside.

9. Add salt, one tablespoon each apple cider vinegar and coconut aminos to the cooking pot. Press the sauté function and cook the sauce until it thickens.

10. After about 10-15 minutes, turn off the Instant Pot. Open and serve the chicken with the sauce. You can garnish with green onion slices.

Nutritional Information Per Serving: Calories 312.6, Fat 28.7g, Carbs 5.0g, Protein 32.5g

9. Salsa Chicken Tacos

Serves: 6

Ingredients

Lettuce wraps

1 cup roasted tomato salsa

½ teaspoon kosher salt

1 teaspoon chili powder

2 lbs. chicken breasts or thighs, boneless and skinless

Directions

1. Arrange the chicken in a single layer in an Instant Pot, and sprinkle the seasoning on both sides. Ensure that the pieces of chicken are in a single layer at the bottom.

2. Pour the salsa on the chicken breast and lock the lid in place. Lock the lid then press the Manual button. Set the timer to 10 minutes for thighs and 7 minutes for chicken breasts.

3. Once the chicken has cooked, release the pressure through quick release to avoid overcooking the chicken. Remove the lid and put the chicken onto a bowl.

4. Shred the chicken using two forks. Taste the cooking liquid and adjust the seasonings accordingly.

5. Now pour the liquid on the chicken and toss to coat. Serve the chicken with lettuce swaps or grain-free tortillas.

6. You can then garnish as desired preferably with taco toppings.

Nutritional Information Per Serving: Calories 201, Fat 5.4g, Carbs 2.9g, Protein 33.4g

10.   Instant Pot Pina Colada Chicken

Serves: 4

Ingredients

2 tablespoons coconut aminos

1/8 teaspoon salt

1 teaspoon cinnamon

1/2 cup coconut cream, full fat

1 cup pineapple chunks, fresh or frozen

2 lbs. chicken thighs cut into 1" pieces

1/2 cup green onion, chopped

Directions

1. Put the ingredients apart from the chopped onions into an instant pot.

2. Close and seal the lid then set to Poultry setting.

3. Once cooked turn off the cooker and allow natural release of pressure for 10 minutes.

4. After the valve drops, gently open the lid and remove the chicken from the pot. Stir and add a teaspoon of arrowroot starch and a tablespoon of water to thicken the sauce.

5. Now press the sauté button and continue to cook until you achieve your desired thickness.

6. Finally turn off the Instant Pot. Serve the chicken with green onion as garnish.

Nutritional Information Per Serving: Calories 320, Fat 24.1g, Carbs 5.2g, Protein 17.9g

11. Delicious Thai Chicken

Serves: 4

Ingredients

¼ cup coconut aminos

½ cup chicken bone broth

½ cup full-fat organic coconut milk

½ teaspoon organic curry powder

1 teaspoon Celtic sea salt

15 small organic mint leaves

2 tablespoons butter or ghee, grass-fed

5 inch stem lemongrass, halved

Zest and juice of 1 lime

2 organic chicken breasts, diced

1 medium red onion, thickly sliced

4 fresh garlic cloves, finely minced or grated

1 inch chunk fresh ginger, grated or finely minced

Directions

1. Using a pair of scissors, cut the chicken meat and set it onto a plate. Then prepare the other ingredients such as lemongrass, lime zest, onion, garlic and ginger.

2. Press the "sauté" button on the instant pot. Add in coconut oil then sauté garlic, ginger and onions for about 5 minutes making sure that you stir the mixture occasionally.

3. Add in chicken and cook until it is no longer pink, say for 2-3 minutes. Press "Keep Warm/Cancel" to turn off the Instant Pot.

4. Now add in lemongrass, coconut milk, lime juice, lime zest, curry powder, mint leaves, coconut aminos and bone broth. Stir to incorporate.

5. Close and lock the lid, ensuring the steam release valve is fully sealed. Set it to "Poultry" and then cook for about 10 minutes.

6. After 10 minutes, turn off the Instant Pot, unplug it and quick release the pressure.

7. Wait until steam venting stops then gently open the lid. Serve with cauliflower rice, garnish with lime wedges, and chopped cilantro.

Nutritional Information Per Serving: Calories 205, 16.3g, Carbs 4.0g, Protein 18.8 g

12. Instant Pot Chicken

Serves: 6

Ingredients

1 tablespoon coconut oil

1 cup water

Seasonings of choice

1 whole chicken

Directions

1. Add a cup of water into an instant pot, and then place a steam rack inside the cooking pot.

2. Heat oil in a large skillet and then cover the chicken with various seasonings.

3. Place the chicken in oil and let the skin sear for 60 seconds on each side and then position the chicken in the steam rack of the cooking pot.

4. Lock the lid and set the cooker to "Chicken" setting and cook the chicken for about 20 minutes. To calculate cooking time, allocate 6 minutes for each pound of the chicken, and then add 2 minutes to the total cook time.

5. Release pressure naturally for 15 minutes.

Nutritional Information Per Serving: Carbs: 1g, Calories: 377.1, Fat: 27g, Protein: 31.2g

13. Instant Pot Chicken Breast salad

Serves: 4

Ingredients

2 cups water

1 1/3 lb. boneless, skinless chicken breast

Brine

60 grams salt

4 cups water

Salad Dressing

6 tablespoons extra virgin olive oil

2 tablespoons balsamic vinegar

2 tablespoons honey

2 tablespoons Dijon mustard

Pinch of Kosher salt

6 cloves garlic, finely minced

Salad

Grape tomatoes, cut in half

Field greens

Directions

1. In a small bowl, mix brine by adding salt to water and mix well.

2. Put the chicken breast in the brine mixture and store in the fridge for about 45 minutes.

3. To cook the chicken, add a cup of water to the Instant Pot. Put your steamer rack in the instant put, then place the chicken on the rack and seal the lid in place.

4. Cook for 5 minutes at high pressure. Turn off the pressure cooker and natural release for about 8 minutes.

5. Carefully open the lid and transfer the chicken to a platter. Ensure that a food thermometer reading for internal temperature is around 161° F – 163° F degrees. If that's not the case, return to the cooking pot for 2-5 minutes but don't cook it again.

6. As soon as internal temperature of 161° F – 163° F is reached, remove from the Instant Pot. Allow the chicken to cool for about 5-10 minutes.

7. To make the salad dressing, mix together minced garlic, balsamic vinegar, honey and Dijon mustard in a small bowl.

8. Add in 3 tablespoons olive oil while stirring. Mix until well incorporated and emulsified.

9. At this point, slice the meat into bite-sized pieces and put them on the grape tomatoes and field greens. Drizzle with honey mustard vinaigrette.

10. Serve the meal either cold or warm.

Nutritional Information Per Serving: Calories 206.3, Fat 11.4g, Carbs 8.1g, Protein 18.3g

14. Chicken and Sauce

Serves: 4

Ingredients

2 teaspoons chicken bouillon

120 ml water

350 ml beer

1/8 teaspoon pepper, freshly ground

2 teaspoons salt

1/2 teaspoon ginger

1 teaspoon cinnamon

1 teaspoon nutmeg

3 chicken breast halves

Preferred sauce

Directions

1. Mix the ginger, cinnamon, nutmeg, salt and pepper and then rub the seasonings onto the meat.

2. Mix together beer, chicken bouillon and water in a separate bowl and then pour into the instant pot.

3. Now add in the chicken and lock the lid. Cook for 20 minutes at high pressure then release the pressure naturally.

4. Set the chicken onto a grill and cook for 10 more minutes.

5. Use barbecue sauce of choice to rub the chicken and grill for 5 minutes. Serve while warm.

Nutritional Information Per Serving: Calories 269.9, Fat 22.6g, Carbs 4.4g, Protein 16.2g

15. Ginger Chicken

Serves: 6

Ingredients

¼ cup water

¼ cup soya sauce

¼ cup dry sherry

1 inch ginger finely grated

1 large onion - finely diced

1 chicken cut into pieces

Directions

1. Press the sauté function on the instant pot and then brown the chicken pieces.

2. Add in the onion, ginger, and mix well followed by soya sauce, sherry and water, and mix well too.

3. Lock the lid and then cook for 6 minutes at manual high pressure.

4. Add in pepper and salt to taste and serve with cauliflower rice.

Nutritional Information Per Serving: Calories: 530, Protein: 19.9g, Carbs: 4.7g, Fat: 10.9gg fat

16. Instant Pot Coq au Vin

Serves: 4

Ingredients

2 tablespoons cognac

Salt & pepper

12-15 radishes or rutabagas

1 cup parsley, chopped

200g small white mushrooms

1 or 2 bay leaves

2 tablespoons almond flour

500ml red wine

2 garlic cloves, crushed

2 medium brown onions, sliced

250g diced (smoked) bacon

¼ cup olive or peanut oil

1 kg chicken pieces

Directions

1. Press the sauté function, add the oil and once it is hot, brown the chicken pieces in batches, and then put aside.

2. Brown the sliced onions and bacon pieces, and add in the chicken, and then sift in the flour

3. Combine the ingredients well and add in cognac if desired.

4. Add in the red wine, and season with salt and pepper. Also add in the bay leaves.

5. Lock the instant pot in place and cook at manual high pressure for 25 minutes.

6. Quick release the pressure 5 minutes before serving then add in the mushrooms. Close and cook for 5 minutes.

7. In a separate cooker, steam the potatoes and serve with the chicken garnished with parsley.

Nutritional Information Per Serving: Calories: 274, Carbs: 11g, Fat: 21g, Protein: 18g

17. Instant Pot Chicken with Duck Sauce

Serves: 4

Ingredients

¼ cup chicken broth

¼ cup white wine

½ teaspoon dried marjoram

½ teaspoon paprika

Salt and pepper to taste

3 pound whole chicken, cut into pieces

1 tablespoon olive oil

For Duck Sauce:

2 tablespoons honey

1 ½ teaspoons fresh ginger root, minced

2 tablespoons white vinegar

¼ cup apricot preserves

Directions

1. Press the sauté function on your instant pot and then add in the oil.

2. Once hot, add in the chicken and brown on all the sides, and then remove it from the cooking pot.

3. Season the chicken with marjoram, salt, pepper and paprika. Drain and discard any fat accumulated in the Instant Pot.

4. Now mix in chicken broth and wine, and scrap bits of food stuck in the instant pot.

5. Return the chicken back into the instant pot, seal the lid in place and cook at manual high pressure for 8 minutes.

6. Quick release the pressure, open the lid and if the chicken has cooked through, the internal temperature should be at 180 degrees F.

7. Transfer the chicken to a plate and add vinegar, honey, apricot preserves and ginger to the instant pot.

8. Lock the lid in place and cook for around 10 minutes at high pressure. Quick release the pressure and you will have a thick syrupy sauce.

9. Spoon the thick sauce over the chicken and serve.

Nutritional Information Per Serving: Calories 164, Fat 10g, Carbs 6g, Protein 21g

18.Coca Cola Chicken

Serves: 4

Ingredients

Salt & pepper

2 tablespoons olive oil

500 ml Coca Cola

1 small chopped chili

1 tablespoon balsamic vinegar

1 large finely onion, chopped

4 chicken drumsticks

Directions

1. Press the sauté function and add in some oil. Once hot, add in the chicken pieces to brown.

2. Remove from heat and then add the onion to the cooker to brown in the juices.

3. Then add in the chili, balsamic vinegar and Coca-Cola.

4. Return the chicken to the cooker and season to taste. Seal the instant pot and cook for 10 minutes at manual high pressure.

5. Release the pressure naturally and serve with some vegetables.

Nutritional Information Per Serving: Calories 202.4, Fat 5.7g, Carbs 3.6g, Protein 17.2g

19. Garlic & Onion Chicken

Serves: 6 - 8

Ingredients

2 lbs. boneless skinless chicken breasts

½ teaspoon salt

1 tablespoon garlic, chopped

1 cup chicken broth

1 small yellow onion, chopped

Directions

1. Add the chicken, broth, salt, garlic and onion into an Instant Pot and cook for 12 minutes at high pressure for thawed chicken and 20 minutes for frozen chicken.

2. Quick release the pressure, remove the chicken breasts and put on a cutting board or a plate. Shred the mea using a fork.

3. Remove two thirds of the liquid from the cooking pot then return the meat to the pot. Stir to coat with the sauce then serve.

Nutritional Information Per Serving: Calories 170.9, Fat 1g, Carbs 0.1g, Protein 32g

20. Salsa Verde Chicken

Serves: 6

Ingredients

2 lbs. chicken breasts

1 cup salsa Verde

¾ cup onion

Directions

1. Add the chicken, salsa Verde and the onion to the instant pot, then cook thawed meat for 12 minutes at high pressure. If the chicken is frozen, cook for 20 minutes.

2. Quick release pressure by turning the pressure valve to "Vent". Then transfer the chicken breast to a cutting board or plate. Use two forks to shred the chicken.

3. Remove around two-thirds of the cooking liquid from the pot. Then return the shredded meat to the Instant Pot and stir to coat with the remaining liquid.

4. To serve, top the shredded chicken with green onions.

Nutritional Information Per Serving: Calories: 185; Fat: 10g; Protein: 13g, Carbs: 9g

21. Lemon Garlic Chicken

Serves: 4

Ingredients

3 teaspoons arrowroot flour

1 large lemon juiced

1/4 teaspoon paprika

1 teaspoon dried parsley

1/2 cup organic chicken broth or homemade

5 garlic cloves, minced

1 tablespoon avocado oil, lard, or ghee

1 onion, diced

1 teaspoon sea salt

2 lbs. pounds chicken breasts or thighs

Directions

1. Press the sauté button on the instant pot and allow to get hot. Then add in cooking fat and diced onion.

2. Cook the ingredients until softened, say for 5 to 10 minutes.

3. Add the rest of the ingredients apart from the arrowroot flour then cover and secure the lid in place.

4. Set the pressure cooker to "poultry" setting and then cook the chicken until the beep sounds.

5. Quick release steam and then carefully open the lid.

6. Thicken the sauce with the arrowroot powder to desired consistency. Just get about ¼ cup of the sauce and add in the arrowroot then pour it back into the cooking pot.

7. Stir and serve the chicken immediately.

Nutritional Information Per Serving: Calories 150.3, Fat 9.9g, Carbs 7.6g, Protein 8.9g

Chpater 3: Meat Recipes

22.   Lamb Curry

Serves: 6

Ingredients

1 medium zucchini, diced

3 medium carrots, sliced

1 medium onion, diced

1 ½ tablespoons yellow curry powder

1 (14 ounce) can diced tomatoes

1 tablespoon ghee

Pinch of black pepper + to taste

¼ teaspoon sea salt + to taste

Juice of ½ lime

½ cup coconut milk

1-inch piece fresh ginger, grated

4 cloves garlic, minced

1 ½ lbs. cubed lamb stew meat

¾ teaspoon turmeric, optional

Cilantro, chopped (optional)

Directions

1. Mix coconut milk, meat, grated ginger, minced garlic, pepper, salt and lime juice in a container and marinate the meat for about 30-60 minutes.

2. Once ready, mix the marinated meat with ghee, tomatoes and their juice, curry powder, carrots and onions in an instant pot.

3. Lock and secure the lid then set to Manual. Cook on high for about 20 minutes.

4. After 20 minutes, let the Instant Pot to release pressure naturally for around 15 minutes. Release the remaining steam by flipping the steam release handle to 'Venting'.

5. Open the lid and then set the Instant Pot to sauté. Then add in diced zucchini and simmer the mixture for 5-6 minutes or until the sauce is slightly thickened and the zucchini is tender.

6. Serve the lamb curry with cauliflower rice garnished with chopped cilantro.

Nutritional Information Per Serving: Calories: 230, Fat: 9g, Carbs: 11g, Protein: 25g

23.　Instant Pot Pork and Kraut

Serves: 4

Ingredients

1 cup filtered water

3 cloves garlic peeled & sliced

2 large onions sliced or chopped

2 tablespoons organic coconut oil or ghee

2-3 lbs. pork roast

Freshly Ground Black Pepper

4-6 cups sauerkraut, divided

Sea salt

Optional

1 lb. hot dogs nitrate free, grass fed beef

½ lb. kielbasa nitrate free, grass fed beef

Directions

1. Season the pork shoulder with pepper and salt and then set aside.

2. Brown the pork roast in a large skillet with coconut oil then brown it on all sides over high heat, including on the edges.

3. Put the browned pork roast in the cooking pot of your instant pot. Add garlic, water, onions and season with additional salt and pepper.

4. Cook the meat on Meat/Stew function for approximately 35 minutes.

5. Naturally release pressure and then add in half of the sauerkraut and save the rest to be eaten raw to help preserve beneficial bacteria (probiotics).

6. Cook the mixture at high pressure for about 5 minutes to flavor the meat. In case the meat is tough, you may need to cook it for 15 minutes!

7. Quick release the pressure and then add in kielbasa and hot dogs if using.

8. Cook for about 5 minutes at high pressure but not for longer as this might break the hot dogs apart.

9. Quick release pressure and then allow the food to rest for a few minutes. Serve with raw sauerkraut and enjoy.

Nutritional Information Per Serving: Calories 295.6, Fat 4.3g, Carbs 17.9g, Protein 6.0g

24.   Meatballs in the Instant Pot

Serves: 5

Ingredients

3 cups marinara sauce

1 teaspoon olive oil

1/3 cup warm water

¼ teaspoon dried oregano

1 teaspoon dried onion flakes

¼ teaspoon garlic powder

¼ teaspoon ground black pepper

1 teaspoon kosher salt

2 eggs

½ cup almond flour

¾ cup grated parmesan cheese

2 tablespoon fresh parsley, chopped

1.5 lbs. ground beef

Directions

1. Mix the ingredients except the marinara and olive oil in a medium bowl.

2. From this mixture, make 15 two-inch meatballs and put aside.

3. Now coat the bottom of the cooking pot using olive oil and use the sauté function to brown the meatballs on all sides.

4. Once done, layer the meatballs in the cooking pot and leave a ½ inch of space between each ball. Make sure you don't press them down.

5. Pour the sauce over the meatballs and secure the lid in place. Set the instant pot on manual and select low pressure and cook for 10 minutes.

6. As soon as the beep sounds, quick release to prevent further cooking. Then carefully open the lid and serve the meatballs with sauce.

Nutritional Information Per Serving: Calories: 455, Fat: 33g, Carbs: 5g, Protein 34g

25.   Instant Pot Barbacoa Beef

Serves: 4-5

Ingredients

2 bay leaves

½ teaspoon oil

Black pepper

1 1/4 teaspoons kosher salt

1 1/3 lbs. beef bottom round roast, all fat trimmed

1/2 cup water

¼ teaspoon ground cloves

½ tablespoon ground oregano

1/2 tablespoon ground cumin

1-2 tablespoon chiptoles in adobo sauce

½ lime, juice

¼ medium onion

2-3 cloves garlic

Directions

1. Put cloves, chipotles, oregano, cumin, lime juice, onion, garlic and water in a blender. Puree the ingredients until well incorporated.

2. Cut the chuck roast into 3-inch pieces and season with black pepper and salt.

3. Press the sauté button and add in the oil. Brown the chuck roast in batches on all sides in around 5 minutes or so.

4. Add in the sauce you have already blended along with bay leaves. Cover and cook for 65 minutes at high pressure.

5. Once the time elapses, remove from the cooking pot and put in a dish. Using two forks shred the meat and reserve the liquids.

6. Return the roast to the cooking pot and add about 1 ½ cups of the reserved liquid, ½ teaspoon cumin and ½ teaspoon salt to taste.

7. Stir and serve.

Nutritional Information Per Serving: Calories: 153, Fat: 4.5g, Carbs: 2g, Protein: 24g

26.   Pork & Cauliflower Rice

Serves: 4

Ingredients

1/2 teaspoon salt

1 tablespoon cumin

1 tablespoon oregano

1 teaspoon turmeric

1 tablespoon animal fat

3 cloves garlic, sliced

1 tablespoon lime juice

2 green onions, sliced

1/2 cup cilantro, divided

1/2 red onion, sliced

1/2 cup bone broth

4 cups riced cauliflower

1 lb. pork belly, cooked and cubed

Directions

1. Put all ingredients in an Instant Pot apart from cilantro.

2. Lock the lid and press the manual button then set the timer to 15 minutes.

3. Once the timer goes off, release pressure naturally for about 10 minutes then open the lid and serve.

27.   Mexican Beef

Serves: 4-6

Ingredients

2 radishes, thinly sliced

½ cup minced cilantro

freshly ground black pepper

½ teaspoon Fish Sauce

½ cup bone broth

½ cup roasted tomato salsa

6 garlic cloves, peeled and smashed

1 tablespoon tomato paste

1 medium onion, thinly sliced

1 tablespoon ghee

1½ teaspoons kosher salt

1 tablespoon chili powder

2½ lbs. boneless beef, cut into 2-inch cubes

Directions

1. Mix chili powder, salt and cubed beef in a bowl. Press the sauté function then add ghee to the cooking pot. Once ghee has melted; sauté onions until translucent.

2. Stir in garlic and tomato paste, and then cook until fragrant, say for 30 seconds.

3. Now toss in seasoned beef, along with salsa, fish sauce and stock. Then secure the lid in place.

4. Press the "Meat/Stew" button and cook for about 30-35 minutes.

5. Once ready, release the pressure naturally for about 15 minutes. Then open the lid and season as desired.

6. Top the stew with radishes or cilantro and serve.

Nutritional Information Per Serving: Calories 235.1, Fat 12.5g, Carbs 8.3g, Protein 12.8g

28. French Dip Sandwich

Serves: 4-5

Ingredients

½ loaf Paleo bread

¾ cups beef stock

1 teaspoon onion powder

½ tablespoon minced garlic

½ tablespoon Worcestershire sauce

½ teaspoon pepper, freshly ground

¾ teaspoons salt

3 lbs. chuck roast

Directions

1. Put beef stock, onion powder, garlic, sauce, pepper and salt in an Instant Pot, and set the timer to 1 hour if meat is thawed and 1 ½ hours if frozen.

2. Cook at high pressure until the meat cooked through.

3. Separate the meat and juices by passing the mixture through a mesh strainer over a pot. Put the meat in a bowl and use a fork to shred it.

4. Press sauté function and let the juices simmer until they have reduced by half. Skim of any fat that rises to the top.

5. At this point, season with salt and pepper, and then cut the bread into sandwich sizes and split down its center.

6. Put the shredded meat onto the bread and top with provolone cheese. Put on a cookie sheet and melt the provolone under a broiler until bubbly.

7. Finally assemble the sandwich and ladle the sauce in container to make a dip. Serve the sandwich and enjoy.

Nutritional Information Per Serving: Calories: 237, Fat: 13g, Carbs: 1g, Protein: 27g

29.   Instant Pot Maple Smoked Brisket

Serves: 4

Ingredients

3 fresh thyme sprigs

1 tablespoon liquid smoke

2 cups bone broth or stock

½ teaspoon smoked paprika

1 teaspoon onion powder

1 teaspoon mustard powder

1 teaspoon black pepper

2 teaspoons smoked sea salt

2 tablespoons maple or coconut sugar

1.5 lb. beef brisket

Directions

1. Remove frozen brisket from the fridge 30 minutes earlier, pat it dry with paper towels and set it aside.

2. Prepare the spice blend by mixing paprika, onion powder, mustard powder, pepper, smoked sea salt and maple sugar. Season the meat on all sides.

3. Press the sauté button on the Instant Pot and let it heat up for 2-3 minutes. Coat the bottom of the cooking pan with cooking oil and add in the meat.

4. Brown the brisket on all sides until golden. Then turn it fatty side up and add thyme, liquid smoke and the broth. Scrape off any browned bits off the bottom and lock the lid.

5. Switch to "manual" then set it at high pressure for 50 minutes. Once ready, natural release pressure and then transfer the mat to a plate then cover with foil.

6. Press the sauté button on the Instant Pot to thicken the sauce with lid off for around 10 minutes.

7. Finally slice the brisket and serve it with veggies of choice. Drizzle with the sauce and enjoy.

Nutritional Information Per Serving: Calories: 284.6, Fat: 16.2g, Carbs: 10.6g, Protein: 23.2g

30. Chunk Roast & Gravy

Serves: 4-6

Ingredients

6 cloves garlic, peeled

4 carrots, peeled or scrubbed

2 parsnips, peeled

4 three inch sprigs thyme

1 3-inch sprig rosemary

2 teaspoons fish sauce

2 tablespoons balsamic vinegar

1 1/2 cups beef broth

Black pepper, freshly ground

A good pinch of salt

4 lbs. chuck roast, cut into 4 pieces

Parsley, chopped

Directions

1. Season the meat with salt and pepper and put in an Instant Pot.

2. Put the rest of the ingredients in the cooking pot, lock the lid in place and set the timer to 1 hour at high pressure.

3. Once ready, natural release pressure for about 15 minutes.

4. Remove the roast from the pot and set on a plate and the veggies into a blender while discarding the thyme and rosemary stems.

5. Pour the liquid from the Instant Pot into a measuring cup or a large jar. Remove any fat using a small ladle or large spoon.

6. Pour the rest of the liquid into the blender with the veggies and puree until smooth. If need be, season the mixture with salt and pepper.

7. Using two forks shred the meat and pour gravy on the meat. Alternatively, you can stir gravy into the roast.

8. Serve the roast with cauliflower mash or other roasted or mashed root veggie.

Nutritional Information Per Serving: Calories 327.9, Fat 25.6g, Carbs 1.8g, Protein 22.9 g

31. Pressure Cooker Beef Chili

Serves: 4

Ingredients

1 teaspoon garlic powder

1 teaspoon paprika

4 teaspoons chili powder

1 tablespoon Worcestershire sauce

1 tablespoon fresh parsley, chopped

1 teaspoon onion powder

1 teaspoon sea salt

½ teaspoon ground black pepper

26 oz. finely chopped tomatoes

4 large carrots, chopped small

1 large onion, diced

1 green bell pepper, seeded and diced

1 lb. grass-fed organic beef

Pinch of cumin

Sliced jalapenos, optional

Diced onions, optional

Dairy-free sour cream, optional

Directions

1. Press the sauté setting, then add ground beef to the instant pot and cook until brown.

2. Add the rest of the ingredients and mix well. Cover, lock the lid and cook on Meat/Stew function for 35 minutes.

3. Once cooked, quick release or natural release pressure and serve.

Nutritional Information Per Serving: Calories: 222, Fat: 7g, Carbs 11g, Protein: 27g

32.   Instant Pot Mojo Pork Shoulder

Serves: 4-6

Ingredients

Fresh cilantro, chopped

3 lbs. boneless pork shoulder, cut into 2-inch cubes

1/2 teaspoon cumin, ground

1 teaspoon salt

5 cloves garlic, minced

1/4 cup lime juice

1/4 cup orange juice

Spicy Slaw for serving

For the Slaw:

1/4 small red onion, thinly sliced

1 bell pepper, thinly sliced

1 small jalapeño, quartered, thinly sliced

1/2 head green cabbage, shredded

1/2 teaspoon coriander, ground

1 tablespoon apple cider vinegar

2 tablespoons avocado oil

1/4 cup lime juice

Pinch of salt

Directions

1. Mix cumin, salt, garlic, lime juice and orange juice in the insert of your Instant Pot.

2. Add the pork and toss to coat. If desired, you can marinate the pork overnight in the fridge to make it more flavorful.

3. Close and seal the lid after ensuring that the rubber seal is inside the lid. Cook for about 45 minutes at high pressure.

4. Once cooking is over, press the Keep Warm / Cancel function and allow the pressure to release for 10 minutes. Then turn the nozzle to venting to remove any remaining pressure.

5. At this point, preheat the broiler. Remove the pork from the pot and set onto a baking sheet.

6. Press the sauté function on the Instant Pot and cook the liquid for up to 15 minutes to reduce it to about 1 cup. Once the stew has thickened, transfer to a heat-proof bowl and then skin off floating fat as it cools down.

7. Meanwhile, broil the pork for around 3-5 minutes on each side until brown and crispy. Turn several times to brown each of the sides.

8. Serve the pork shoulder with the sauce or slaw. To prepare the slaw, mix together coriander, apple cider vinegar, avocado oil, lemon juice and salt in a large bowl.

9. Mix the remaining ingredients using your hands, and break them down as you squeeze them.

10. Season with vinegar and lime juice. Serve.

Nutritional Information Per Serving: Calories 120.2, Fat 5.3g, Carb 11.3g, Protein 8.0g

33.   Instant Pot Quiche

Serves: 4

Ingredients

1 cup parmesan Cheese

2 large green onions, chopped

1/2 cup diced ham

1 cup ground sausage, cooked

4 slices cooked and crumbled bacon

1/8 teaspoon black pepper, ground

1/4 teaspoon salt

1/2 cup almond or coconut milk

6 large eggs, beaten

Directions

1. Put a metal rivet in your instant pot and then add water into the instant pot.

2. Whisk together milk, eggs, salt and pepper in a large bowl. Then add in ham, sausage, bacon, cheese and green onions to a soufflé dish and mix.

3. Now pour the egg mixture over the meat, and stir to incorporate. Cover the soufflé dish loosely with aluminum foil.

4. Drop the dish into the trivet of the cooking pot using an aluminum sling. Lock the lid and cook for 30 minutes at high pressure.

5. Once cooked, turn off; allow to cool for 10 minutes then quick release. Open the lid and remove the foil.

6. Serve. You can sprinkle some additional cheese then broil to melt and lightly brown.

Nutritional Information Per Serving: Calories: 301, Carbs: 17g, Fat 10g, Protein: 31g

34. Pressure Cooker Beef Ribs

Serves: 4

Ingredients

2 tablespoons white wine or vodka

1 tablespoon salt

3 tablespoons of tamari sauce

1 cup water

1 onion, diced

2 tablespoons curry powder

1 tablespoon Szechuan peppercorns, if desired

2 lb. boneless beef short ribs

6 star anise, optional

Directions

1. Put all the ingredients in an Instant Pot, then set the pressure cooker to Meat/Stew setting.

2. Turn on the cooker and cook for 45 minutes. Serve when cooked through.

Nutritional Information Per Serving: Calories: 174, Fat: 6g, Carbs: 8g, Protein: 22g

35.   Cranberry Pot Roast

Serves: 4-6

Ingredients

2 cups bone broth, home made

6 whole cloves

2 large garlic cloves, peeled

1 3-inch cinnamon stick

1 teaspoon horseradish powder

¼ cup honey

½ cup water

1 cup whole cranberries, fresh or frozen

½ cup white wine

1 3-4 pound beef arm roast

Salt and pepper

2 tablespoons olive oil

Directions

1. Using paper towels, pat dry the meat then season with salt and pepper.

2. Press sauté button on the Instant Pot and heat the oil. Then brown the roast for 8-10 minutes on all sides. Remove from heat and set aside.

3. Into the empty pot, pour in wine and then scrape up the brown bits using a wooden spoon. Cook for about 4-5 minutes, stirring often to deglaze the pan.

4. Then add in honey, cinnamon stick, whole cloves, garlic, honey, water and horseradish powder. Cook the mixture for 4-5 minutes or until the cranberries begin to burst.

5. Return the beef to pot and nestle it into the cranberries. Add broth to almost cover the meat.

6. Lock the lid and cook for 75 minutes at high pressure. Then natural pressure release for 15 minutes and open the lid.

7. Transfer the meat to a serving dish, and drizzle cranberry sauce over top.

Nutritional Information Per Serving: Calories 327.9, Fat 25.6g, Carbs 3.8g, Protein 24g

36. Breakfast Sandwich

Serves: 1

Ingredients

2 slices gluten-free bread

1 tablespoon Cheddar Cheese, grated

1 egg

1 thin slice of prosciutto

1/16 teaspoon olive oil

1 cup water

Directions

1. Add a cup of water into the instant pot and then put in a steamer tray or trivet.

2. Into the bottom of a ramekin, place a little amount of coconut oil, butter, or olive oil and evenly coat its insides.

3. Now into the bottom of the ramekin, put a slice of prosciutto and then add in the egg or egg substitute. Follow this with cracked pepper and then sprinkle shredded cheese on top.

4. Use a piece of tin foil to cover the ramekin, and set it into the steamer basket. Now insert the basket into the cooker's pot just on top of the trivet.

5. Close the cooker and lock the lid in place, then cook at low pressure for 6 minutes.

6. Once ready, release the pressure naturally for around 5 minutes.

7. Meanwhile, toast the rye bread slices. Once ready, open the instant pot and remove the steamer basket.

8. Remove the ramekin and run a butter knife through the edge of the egg creation. Tip it out and set onto the slice of rye. Serve instantly

Nutritional Information Per Serving: Calories: 321, carbs: 11g, Fat: 3g, Protein: 6.8g

37.   Instant Pot Pork

Serves: 4-5

Ingredients

¼ cup water

½ tablespoon liquid smoke

½ teaspoon fish sauce

¼ cup diced pineapple

½ teaspoon sea salt

½ tablespoon lard or bacon fat

2-3 lb. pork shoulder

Directions

1. Press the sauté button and wait for the Instant Pot to display HOT. Then cut the pork into two pieces, and add lard to the cooking pot.

2. Sear each half of the pork shoulder for 2-3 minutes on each side. Once well browned, remove from the cooking pot and turn off the cooker.

3. Sprinkle salt on the meat, and add in fish sauce, pineapple, water and liquid smoke.

4. Press the Manual button and set the timer to 90 minutes. Once the timer beeps, release the pressure naturally.

5. Now remove the pork from the cooking pot and transfer the juices into a jar. Using two forks pull the meat apart to remove any excess fat.

6. Remove the fat from atop of the jar and discard. If desired, add some of the juices to the pork.

Nutritional Information Per Serving: Calories: 284.6, Fat:16.2g, Carbs: 10.6g, Protein: 23.2g

38.   Corned Beef & Cabbage

Serves: 6

Ingredients

1 head cabbage, cut into wedges

5 medium carrots, cut into chunks

1½ lbs. red potatoes, small or medium

1 teaspoon dried thyme

½ teaspoon whole allspice berries

3 whole black peppercorns

2 bay leaves

3 garlic cloves, peeled and smashed

1 small onion, peeled and quartered

4 cups water

3-4 lbs. corned beef brisket

Directions

1. Put corned beef, thyme, allspice, peppercorns, garlic cloves, onion quarters and water in an Instant Pot, then lock the lid.

2. Set the cooker to Manual for 90 minutes and then cook.

3. Once the time elapses, switch off the Instant Pot and let the pressure release naturally in about 10 minutes.

4. Take out the meat from the liquid and set onto a plate. Cover the meat using a tin foil, and let it cool for around 15 minutes. Meanwhile, prepare the veggies.

5. Once ready, add in cabbage, carrot and potato to the liquid in the pressure cooker and secure the lid. Set it to manual and cook for around 10 minutes.

6. Quick release the pressure and carefully open the lid. Remove the veggies using a slotted spoon.

7. Serve the veggies with corned beef. You can moisten the veggies and meat with the cooking liquid.

Nutritional Information Per Serving: Calories: 318, Fat: 15.8g, Carbs: 1.6g, Protein: 39.4g

40.   Turkey and Gravy

Serves: 6

Ingredients

1 bay leaf

1½ cups bone broth

¼ cup dry white wine

2 teaspoons dried sage

1 garlic clove, peeled and smashed

1 celery rib, diced

1 large carrot, diced

1 medium onion, diced

2 tablespoons ghee or coconut oil

Black pepper

Salt

1 4-5 lb. bone-in, skin-on turkey breast

1 tablespoon tapioca starch, optional

Directions

1. Pat-dry the meat and season with pepper and salt. Press the sauté function on the instant pot, add in the ghee to melt.

2. Once melted, add in the turkey breast to brown with the skin side down for about 5 minutes. Transfer to a plate, but leave the melted fat in the cooking pot.

3. Add in celery root, carrot and onion to the pot and cook on sauté function. Cook for around 5 minutes then stir in sage and garlic. Cook for about 30 seconds, until fragrant.

4. At this point, pour in the wine and cook for about 3 minutes, or until slightly reduced.

5. Stir in bay leaf and broth and scrape up browned bits stuck onto the pot's bottom using a wooden spoon.

6. Put the turkey skin side up into the Instant Pot along with accumulated juices. Lock and secure the lid in place and cook for 35 minutes at high pressure.

7. Once done, quick release the pressure and gently open the lid. Put the turkey breast onto a plate or carving board.

8. Cover it loosely with foil, and let it cool down as you make the gravy.

9. To prepare the gravy, transfer the veggies and the cooking liquid into a blender and process until smooth.

10. Return the gravy to the pot and cook until thickened. Once reduced to around 2 cups turn off the cooker and add seasonings.

11. In case you like thick gravy, mix a tablespoon of tapioca starch with a tablespoon of warm water and whisk into the gravy.

12. To serve the turkey breast, slice and top with the hot gravy.

Nutritional Information Per Serving: Calories: 330, Carbs: 3.7g, Fat 17.9g, Protein: 38g

41. Instant Pot Lamb Shanks with Butternut Squash

Serves: 6

Ingredients

1/4 teaspoon cardamom, ground

1/2 teaspoon paprika

1/2 teaspoon cumin, ground

1/2 teaspoon cinnamon

1/8 teaspoon cayenne pepper

1 teaspoon curry powder

2 tablespoons ghee

1 teaspoon kosher sea salt

1 butternut squash, halved and seeded

3/4 teaspoon black pepper, freshly ground

1 1/2 teaspoons kosher sea salt

2 cups beef stock

1 cup robust red wine

4 sprigs fresh thyme

1 tablespoon rosemary, chopped

6 ounce can tomato paste

1 medium onion, diced

1 large carrot, cut into 1/4" dice

2 - 1 1/2 pounds lamb shanks

1 tablespoon olive oil

4 tablespoons ghee, divided

8 ounces shallots, thinly sliced

Directions

1. Preheat the oven to 375 degrees F. Press sauté function on the instant pot and add ghee. Once melted, add in the shallots and cook for around 20 minutes as you stir occasionally until soft, and then set aside.

2. Heat 2 tablespoons of ghee and olive oil in an Instant Pot. Then brown the lamb shanks for 3 minutes on each side. Remove from cooking pot and set aside.

3. Ass in the onions and carrots, and cook for about 5 minutes. Once the onion softens, add beef stock, wine, tomato paste and pepper.

4. Follow with thyme and rosemary and return the lamb shank mixture to the pot. Lock and cook for 35 minutes at high pressure.

5. Then remove from heat, and allow naturally release of pressure.

6. Fill a baking dish that is large enough to hold the squash halves with about an inch of water Put the squash in the dish, cut sides down. Roast in the preheated oven until tender. After

around 30 minutes, scrape the flesh from the squash into a blender.

7. Add ghee and spices and puree until smooth. Pour into a bowl, cover and keep warm awaiting the lamb shanks.

8. When ready, unlock the lid and remove the shanks. Shred the meat using a fork and discard the bones.

9. Take out the thyme sprigs and ladle some sauce on the lamb to moisten it. Spoon the lamb with remaining sauce and serve.

Nutritional Information Per Serving: Calories: 280, Carbs 10.5g, Fat: 13.8g, Protein: 31.2g

Chapter4: Seafood Recipes

42. Instant Pot Shrimp Paella

Serves: 4

Ingredients

1/4 teaspoon red pepper flakes

1 pinch saffron threads

1/4 teaspoon black pepper

1/2 teaspoon salt

1 teaspoon turmeric

1 teaspoon paprika

1/2 cup white wine

1 cup chicken broth

1 red pepper chopped

4 cloves garlic chopped

1 onion chopped

4 tablespoon butter

1 cup cauliflower rice

1 lb. jumbo shrimp, shell and tail on frozen

1/4 cup cilantro optional

Directions

1. Set the instant pot to Sauté function then add in butter to the pot.

2. Melt the butter and add in onion. Cook until onion has softened.

3. Then add in garlic and cook for about one minute or so. Season the mixture with saffron threads, red pepper flakes, black pepper, turmeric, paprika and salt.

4. Stir the ingredients and cook for a minute or so then add in red peppers.

5. Add in cauliflower rice and cook for a few seconds then add in broth and white wine covering the rice fully.

6. Top with shrimp and turn off the cooker. Cover the mixture and ensure the valve is set to "sealing".

7. Set the instant pot to Manual and select the cook time to 5 minutes then quick release. Open the lid and remove the fish.

8. Peel if you like it and then serve with cilantro.

Nutritional Information Per Serving: Calories 344, Fat 17.49g, Carbs 7.71g, Protein 37.81g

43. 10-Minute Instant Pot Salmon

Serves: 4

Ingredients

1/4 teaspoon black pepper, ground

1/4 teaspoon salt

1 tablespoon butter, unsalted

1 bunch dill weed, fresh

4 fillet salmon

3/4 cup water

3 medium lemon

Directions

1. Put the water and juiced lemon in the bottom of the instant pot then insert the steamer insert.

2. Put the salmon fillets on the steamer insert then sprinkle some fresh dill on top of your salmon fillets and then put a fresh lemon on each of the fillets.

3. Secure the lid in place, set the manual timer to 5 minutes then let cook.

4. As soon as the timer beeps, quick release the steam and then carefully open the lid.

5. Serve the fish with lemon, extra dill and butter. You can also serve with cauliflower rice.

Nutritional Information Per Serving: Calories 382, Fat 15g, Carb 4.3g, Protein 41g

44.   Teriyaki Jumbo Scallops

Serves: 6

Ingredients

1 teaspoon sea salt

1 teaspoon ground ginger

1 teaspoon garlic powder

6 tablespoons 100% maple syrup

1 cup coconut aminos

2 pounds jumbo sea scallops, fresh or thawed from frozen

2 tablespoons avocado oil

Directions

1. Pour 1 tablespoon of the avocado oil into your instant pot and then press on the sauté function.

2. Once the oil is hot, proceed to sear each side of the scallops for about one minute. Meanwhile, whisk together the rest of the ingredients but skip the chives.

3. Now pour the sauce over them and securely lock the lid. Press the Steam function and set cook time to 2 minutes. Let the scallops steam until cooked through.

4. Then quick release pressure and carefully open the lid. Move the scallops to a plate.

5. If you find that the sauce is thin, press the sauté button and let it cook for a few minutes. It should reduce in volume as it thickens.

6. Ladle the sauce over the shellfish and serve garnished with chives.

Nutritional Information Per Serving: Calories 270, Fat 6.05g, Carbs 23.66g, Protein 31.46g

45.   Salmon with Chili-Lime Sauce

Serves 4

Ingredients

Black pepper, freshly ground

Sea salt to taste

2 cups water

4 salmon fillets 5 ounces each

For chili-lime sauce:

1 teaspoon cumin

1 teaspoon paprika

2 tablespoons fresh parsley, chopped

2 tablespoons hot water

2 tablespoons olive oil

2 tablespoons honey

4 cloves garlic minced

2 limes juiced

2 jalapeno seeds removed and diced

Directions

1. In a bowl that has a pourable lip, mix together all the ingredients for sauce and set aside.

2. Then add water to an instant pot and put the fillets on the steam rack inside the cooking pot.

3. Season the fish with salt and pepper then cover and seal the lid. Set the pot to steam mode and set the timer to 5 minutes.

4. As soon as the cooking is finished, quick release the steam to stop further cooking then carefully open the lid.

5. Move the salmon to a serving plate and drizzle with the sauce. Enjoy!

Nutritional Information Per Serving: Calories 155, Fat 9.09g, Carb 13.91g, Protein 6.56g

46.   Fish Coconut Curry

Serves: 4

Ingredients

1/2 teaspoon lime juice

6-8 mint leaves

2-3 sprigs of cilantro

1/2- 1 teaspoon garam masala

1 teaspoon cumin powder

2 teaspoons coriander powder

1/2 teaspoon red chili powder

1/2 teaspoon turmeric powder

1 teaspoon salt

1/2 orange or yellow pepper, sliced

1/2 green pepper, sliced

1/2 medium onion, sliced

10-15 curry leaves

1 tablespoon ginger-garlic paste

1 can coconut milk

1/2 teaspoon mustard seeds

1 tablespoons olive oil

1 lb. tilapia filets, cut in 2 inch pieces

Directions

1. First cut the fish into 2-inch pieces, and then slice the bell peppers and onions.

2. Then finely chop the garlic or pulse a couple of times using a mini-food processor.

3. Press sauté button on the instant pot and wait for 5 minutes. Then add mustard seeds and oil.

4. As soon as the mustard seeds start to splutter, add ginger-garlic paste and curry leaves and sauté for about 30 seconds.

5. Now add in bell peppers and sliced onions and sauté for 30 seconds. Also add the rest of the spices, stir and sauté for additional 30 seconds. Add in coconut milk too and blend well.

6. At this point, bring the mixture to a simmer for a few seconds to avoid coconut milk curdling at high pressure.

7. Add in the fish already cut into 2-inch pieces along with cilantro sprigs and stir well to coat the tilapia with coconut milk. You can also add mint leaves on top to achieve a mild and sweet aroma.

8. Close the lid and seal it in place. On manual setting, set the time to 2-3 minutes, based on the thickness of the fish fillets.

9. Quick release, open the lid and serve the curry with cauliflower rice topped with light squeeze of lime.

Nutritional Information Per Serving: Calories 210, Fat 12g, Carbs 2g, Protein 23g

47.   Pressure-Cooker Octopus

Serves: 6

Ingredients

2 1/2-pound whole octopus, rinsed well

Sea salt

Directions

1. Put the octopus in the instant pot and add sufficient amount of water to cover it.

2. Add large pinches of salt and seal the instant pot. Press the manual option then set the cook time to 15 minutes.

3. Once the 15 minutes lapse, quick release to depressurize the instant pot. Slide a paring knife into the thickest part of the octopus tentacles to check if the octopus is tender. If so, it should slide easily.

4. In case the octopus isn't tender, cook for another 5 minutes. Allow the fish to cool inside the cooking liquid and then drain.

5. To serve, cut out and discard the hard beak found in the center of the base of its body where its tentacles converge.

6. Cut out the section of the head with eyes and discard, and separate the tentacles into individual pieces. These and the other parts are edible.

7. Serve the octopus cold. Just cut the head into pieces and the tentacles too then add it to a salad or other meal and enjoy.

Nutritional Information Per Serving: Calories, 318, Fat, 15.8g, Carbs, 1.6g, Protein 39.4g

48.   Steamed Shrimp and Asparagus

Serves 4

Ingredients

½ tablespoon Cajun seasoning

1 teaspoon olive oil

1 bunch of asparagus

1 pound peeled and deveined shrimp, frozen or fresh

Directions

1. Add a cup of water to the cooking pot of an instant pot. Then insert the steam rack at the bottom.

2. Put the asparagus in a single layer to be the bed for the shell fish. Now place the shrimp on the asparagus.

3. Drizzle with some oil and season with preferred add-ons such as Cajun seasoning.

4. Cover and lock the lid in place. Press on the steam function and set the timer to 2 minutes. If you use fresh shrimp, reduce the time to a minute.

5. Set the pressure to low and set the top knob to sealing. Cook until the instant pot beeps at the end of the cooking.

6. Now move the knob to venting to manually release pressure. Wait until all the pressure has been lost then serve the dish.

Nutritional Information Per Serving: Calories 134, Fat 2.71g, Carbs 1.92g, Protein 23.94g

49.   Instant Pot Mussels Frites

Serves: 4- 6

Ingredients

For frites

3 tablespoons olive oil

1 ½ pounds of gold or russet potatoes

¾ teaspoon black pepper

1 teaspoon salt

1 ½ teaspoons garlic powder

1 tablespoon fresh rosemary, chopped

For mussels

½ cup of fresh flat-leaf parsley, chopped

2 pounds mussels, scrubbed and de-bearded

1 bay leaf

2 cloves garlic, minced

3 roma tomatoes, seeded and chopped

1 cup white wine

For Dipping Sauce

1 clove garlic, minced

2 tablespoons of roasted red pepper, minced

1/3 cup mayonnaise

Directions

1. First preheat the oven to 450 degrees F. Mix together pepper, salt, garlic powder and rosemary in a small bowl.

2. Toss the potatoes with olive oil and the spices on a roasting pan or a large baking sheet.

3. Then roast the mixture in the oven until tender for about 25 to 30 minutes. Remember to stir the mixture once.

4. At this point, mix together garlic, tomatoes, wine and bay leaf in an instant pot. Top the mixture with the mussels.

5. Secure the lid and then close the valve. Press manual then set the cooking time to 3 minutes. Once cooking is done, quick release the pressure.

6. As the mussels cook, mix together the garlic, roasted red pepper and mayonnaise in a small bowl to make the dipping sauce.

7. To serve, top with parsley along with the dipping sauce and mussels.

Nutritional Information Per Serving: Calories: 284.6, Fat: 16.2g, Carbs: 10.6g, Protein: 23.2g

50. Steamed Clams in White Wine Garlic Butter

Serves: 4

Ingredients

1/2 cup flat leaf parsley chopped

Fresh lemon

1 pound fresh radishes trimmed

2 teaspoons seasoning

1 stick butter

1 cup white wine

5 pounds live clams

Directions

1. Begin by washing off the clams and toss any that are opened.

2. Scrub the radishes well and then remove the stems. Trim the radishes tops and slice in half.

3. Now heat an instant pot and then add in radishes and butter. Sauté for about 2 minutes then add in garlic and sauté for a minute.

4. Pour in the wine and heat to reduce for around 3 minutes. Mix in sea salt and then add in the clams and seasoning.

5. Secure the lid and close the valve, then select the steam function. Cook for a minute then natural release pressure.

6. Remove the radish and clams to bowls using slotted spoon or bamboo strainer.

7. Then turn off the instant pot and select Browning or Sauté function. Simmer for 5 minutes and now add in parsley and the rest of butter.

8. Mix well to blend then pour over the clams. Serve and enjoy.

Nutritional Information Per Serving: Calories 293, Fats 21.2g, Carbs 7.6g, Protein 26g

51. Instant Pot Fish in a Packet

Serves 4

Ingredients

4 sprigs of parsley

4 sprigs of thyme

3 small potatoes or radishes, thinly sliced

1 lemon, sliced

1 white onion, chopped

4 fillets of grouper (thawed & drained)

Olive oil

Salt and pepper

Directions

1. First measure the width of your instant pot using a parchment paper to ensure that the end product can fit into the cooking bowl.

2. Just lay a long piece of parchment paper over the instant pot and fold it about 3 centimeters from each side. The parchment creases will act as your pocket guidelines.

3. Thin the onions and radishes using a mandolin on the thinnest settings. Then lay out the parchment paper and layer the ingredients on it.

4. Start with olive oil, radishes or potato slices, salt and paper along with olive oil, fish fillets, salt and pepper and olive oil.

5. Follow with salt, lemon slices, onion, herbs and finish with a swirl of olive oil.

6. Then fold your paper packet and cut a long foil piece. Now wrap the paper packet inside your tin foil.

7. Add 2 cups of water along with the steamer basket to your instant pot. You can cook 2 fillets in each batch or make another layer using another trivet or steamer basket if using a tall instant pot.

8. Ensure there is enough space all round in each packet for the steam to reach them then close the lid. Set the cook time to 10 minutes under high pressure.

9. Once cooking is up, quick release and then open the instant pot. Remove the packets and slide the parchment paper out of the foil on each plate.

10. To serve the fish, just tear the paper open and enjoy.

Nutritional Information Per Serving: Calories 131, Carbs 5g, Fat 3g, Proteins 13g

Quick Seafood Paella

Serves: 4

Ingredients

For Fish Stock

6 cups of water

Bunch of parsley with stems

1 Bay leaf

1 celery

2 carrots

4 white fish heads I used cod

For Paella

2 cups of mixed shellfish, shrimp, mussels and clams

1 cup of seafood squid, scallops, meaty white fish

2 teaspoon sea salt

1/8 teaspoon ground turmeric

1 3/4 cups of seafood stock or vegetable stock

2 cups cauliflower rice

Large pinch saffron threads

1 green bell pepper - diced

1 red bell pepper - diced

1 medium yellow onion diced

4 tablespoons avocado oil

Directions

1. To make the fish stock, just add all the ingredients in the instant pot.

2. Set the cook time to 5 minutes (on the manual setting). As soon as the timer goes off, naturally release pressure.

3. Now make the paella on sauté settings. Heat avocado oil until hot, and then add the peppers. Sauté for about 4 minutes or until the onions softens.

4. Stir in the cauliflower rice, saffron and seafood and now sauté the ingredient for around 2 minutes.

5. Add in salt, turmeric and the stock and blend well. At this point, arrange the shellfish on top without mixing the mixture further.

6. Close and secure the lid then cook for 6 minutes on high pressure.

7. Once cooking is done, naturally release pressure for about 15 minutes, then quick release to remove any remaining pressure.

8. Open the lid and mix the paella well. Then cover and allow to stand for a minute or two and then serve.

Nutritional Information Per Serving: Calories 206.3, Fat 11.4g, Carbs 8.1g, Protein 18.3g

52.   Instant Pot Steamed Crab Legs

Serves: 4

Ingredients

4 tablespoon butter, melted

¾ cup water

Lemon juice

2 lbs. frozen crab legs

Directions

1. Start by placing the steamer basket into the instant pot then put the crab legs on it.

2. Add in water and lock the lid in place.

3. Then press manual and set the timer to 2 minutes. Let it cook until the timer goes off then quick release pressure. The crab meat, once cooked, should be bright pink in color.

4. Combine juice with some melted butter then serve.

Nutritional Information Per Serving: Calories 187.4, Fat 11.9g, Carbs 6.7g, Protein 13.7g

53. Shrimp Creole in an Instant Pot

Serves: 4

Ingredients

1 pound frozen jumbo shrimp (peeled and deveined)

1 bay leaf

1 teaspoon thyme

1/4 teaspoon cayenne pepper

1/2 teaspoon pepper

1 teaspoon salt

1-28 ounce can crushed tomatoes

1 tablespoon tomato paste

2 teaspoons olive oil

2 cloves garlic, minced

2 stalks celery, diced

1 medium onion, chopped

1 bell pepper, diced

Directions

1. Heat olive oil in an Instant pot (use the sauté function) then add in veggies. Sauté until the vegetables begins to soften, or for about 3 minutes.

2. Then add in tomato paste, while stirring for about a minute or so.

3. Now add in the shrimp, seasoning and crushed tomatoes. Stir to blend the ingredients and cover, the valve set to *sealing*.

3. Set the cooker to manual and cook for a minute. Then quick release and check whether the shrimp is fully cooked.

4. Serve over cauliflower rice or set the pot to sauté function if not fully cooked. Just let it cook for a minute or so while stirring.

Nutritional Information Per Serving: Calories 218.1, Fat 10.4g, Carbs 6.4g, Protein 18.3g

54.   Instant Pot Seafood Gumbo

Serves: 8

Ingredients

1 pound medium to large raw shrimp deveined

3/4 cups bone broth

2 bay leaves

1/8 cup tomato paste

14 ounces diced tomatoes

2 celery ribs diced

1 bell pepper diced

1 yellow onion diced

1 ½ tablespoons Cajun or creole seasoning

1 ½ tablespoons ghee or avocado oil

12 ounces sea bass filets cut into 2" chunks

Black pepper

Sea salt

Directions

1. Season the filets with salt and pepper and ensure they are fully coated. Also sprinkle half of the creole or Cajun seasoning and stir to coat.

2. Place the ghee in the instant pot and press the sauté button. Add in the meat chunks and sauté until well cooked on both sides, or for about 4 minutes.

3. Once cooked, move the fish to a large plate using a slotted spoon. Add the remaining Cajon seasoning, celery, pepper and onions to the pot.

4. Sauté the mixture for 2 minutes, or until fragrant. Add in bone broth, bay leaves, tomato paste, diced tomatoes and the cooked fish.

5. Stir and cover the pot. Set the timer to 5 minutes and let the mixture cook. Then quick release pressure by pressing on *venting* setting then remove the lid.

6. Set the pressure cooker to sauté and add in the fish. Cook until the fish is opaque, or for around 3 or 4 minutes.

7. Season with black pepper and sea salt then serve it hot topped with chives and cauliflower rice.

Nutritional Information Per Serving: Calories 191, Carbs 10g, Protein 14g, Fat 5g

55. Instant Pot Salmon Casserole

Serves 4

Ingredients

1 can of cream of celery soup

2 cups frozen vegetables

1 teaspoon of minced garlic

Ground pepper to taste

1/4 cup olive oil

2 frozen salmon pieces

2 cups almond milk

2 cups chicken broth

A shake of ground parmesan

Preferred low carb spices

Directions

1. Heat olive oil in an instant pot, using the sauté function, then add in salmon. Cook until defrosted enough to split apart and white on both sides.

2. Add in garlic and stir into olive oil. Deglaze the pot with chicken soup. Add in vegetables, almond milk and the spices, stir.

3. Top with the celery soup and stir so as to mix well and not to be clumpy. Lock the lid in place and cook for 8 minutes.

4. Quick release and serve.

Nutritional Information Per Serving: Carbs 5.1g, Calories 384, Fat 23.0g Protein: 26.4g

56. Salmon with Lemon & Dill

Serves 4

Ingredients

Fresh veggies, as side dish

3 teaspoon fresh dill, chopped

1/4 cup + 3 teaspoon lemon juice, divided

Salt and pepper

1 lb. salmon fillet, cut into 3 pieces

Directions

1. Add a cup of water along with lemon juice to the Instant Pot. Put the fish pieces on the steam rack with the skin side facing down.

2. Season the salmon with pepper and salt. Then drizzle a teaspoon of lemon juice onto each fillet.

3. Now sprinkle dill on the fish and secure the lid. Press manual then set the timer to 2 minutes and cook the salmon fillets until the beep sounds.

4. After the beep, natural release accumulated pressure then serve with cauliflower rice and veggies.

Nutritional Information Per Serving: Calories 168, Fat 6g, Carbs 5g, Protein 12g

57.Spicy Lemon Salmon

Serves: 4

Ingredients

1 cup water

1-2 tablespoons chili pepper

2 lemons juice one and slice the other one

3-4 Wild Sockeye Salmon fillets

Pepper

Sea Salt, to taste

Directions

1. First season the fish with salt, pepper and lemon juice.

2. Then insert eh steam rack into the cooking pot and put the salmon fillets on the rack in a single layer.

3. Pour any remaining seasonings and lemon juice over the fish. Add a cup of water to the Instant Pot taking care not to wash away the seasonings.

4. Cover and seal the lid in place. Set the timer to 5 minutes though this depends on the size of the fillets. You should reduce cooking time by a minute for every ¼" smaller than 1 inch and increase time by 1 minute for every ¼" larger than 1 inch of the fillet.

5. After cooking is done, manually release pressure and wait until all pressure has escaped before opening the lid. Serve.

Nutritional Information Per Serving: Calories 284.6, Fat 1.2g, Carbs 2.6g, Protein 23.2g

58. Instant pot Steamed Clams

Serves 4-6

Ingredients

2 pounds of clams

2 teaspoons of minced garlic

½ cup of water

½ cup of white wine

Directions

1. Add water and wine to the instant pot along with garlic. Combine well.

2. Put the clams on the steamer tray and set the timer to 4 minutes. Set the vent to "sealing".

3. As soon as cooking is over, quick release pressure and open the lid.

4. Serve the dish with a bowl of cooking sauce or side of butter.

Nutritional Information Per Serving: Calories 213, Protein 26.7g, Fat 3.4g, Carbs 2.5g

59. Mediterranean-style Cod

Serves 6

Ingredients

1- 28 ounce can diced tomatoes

1 teaspoon oregano

1/2 teaspoon black pepper

1 teaspoon salt

1 onion, sliced

1 lemon, juiced

3 tablespoons butter

6 pieces of frozen or fresh cod

Directions

1. Set the cooker to sauté to melt the butter then add the other ingredients.

2. Stir to blend then sauté for about 8 to 10 minutes.

3. Layer the fish portions in the sauce, and cover each piece of fish with sauce using a spoon.

4. Now seal the lid and cook for about 5 minutes for frozen fish and 3 minutes for fresh fish.

5. After the beep sounds, quick release and then carefully open the lid. Serve the cod with sauce and enjoy.

Nutritional Information Per Serving: Calories 208, Fat 4g, Carbs 5g, Protein 18g

60. Perfectly Steamed Mussels

Serves 4

Ingredients

½ Cup of water

½ cup dry white wine

1 clove of garlic, smashed

1 lb. Of baby spinach

1 small head of radicchio, cut into thin strips

1 white onion, chopped

2 lbs. Mussels, cleaned and de-bearded

Olive oil

Directions

1. To clean the mussels' shells, simply scrub using a scrubby sponge or nylon brush.

2. Lay a single layer of baby spinach and radicchio strips on serving plates and set aside.

3. Press sauté button and add olive oil into Instant Pot. Then add garlic and onion and cook until softened.

4. Then de-glaze with white or red wine and immediately add the steamer basket with the mussels. Seal the lid.

5. Cook on low pressure for 1 minute then quick release pressure.

6. Divide the mussel between the spinach layered plates and ladle the steaming liquid over the mussels. .

Nutritional Information Per Serving: Calories 298, Fats 7.2g, Carbs 7.6g, Protein 26g

Chapter 5: Fruits and Veggies Recipes

61.Sweet and Orangey Brussels Sprouts

Serves 8

Ingredients

½ teaspoon salt or to taste

1/4 teaspoon black pepper, or to taste

2 tablespoons maple syrup

1 tablespoon Earth Balance buttery spread

1 teaspoon grated orange zest

1/4 cup freshly squeezed orange juice

2 pounds Brussels sprouts (1.5 pounds when trimmed)

Directions

1. Trim Brussels sprouts and rinse under cold water.

2. Add all ingredients into the instant pot then cover making sure that the quick release switch is actually closed.

3. Next, press the manual button, set the time to 3-4 minutes if the sprouts are whole and of good size and 2-3 minutes if the sprouts are small and cut into half. You can reduce the time if you like them harder.

4. When the time lapses, press the off button then proceed to release pressure using the quick release method.

5. Stir well until the sauce covers the Brussels sprouts then serve.

Nutritional Information Per Serving: Calories 65, 2g Fat, Protein 3g, Carbs 12g

62.   Pressure Cooker Collard Greens

Serves: 4

Ingredients

1 teaspoon sugar

1/2 teaspoon salt

1 tablespoon balsamic vinegar

3 minced garlic cloves

1 small onion, sliced thin

2 tablespoons diced tomatoes /2 tablespoons tomato puree

2 tablespoons olive oil

1/2 cup chicken broth

1 bunch fresh collard greens

Directions

1. Soak the collard greens for about 30 minutes in a sink filled with water to remove dirt.

2. Mix the tomato puree, garlic, chicken broth, vinegar, oil and onion in the instant pot and then stir thoroughly to combine all the ingredients.

3. Then remove the soaked greens from the water one by one ensuring that you don't disturb the water to keep dirt at the bottom while the greens float.

4. Chop the thick stems that are at the base of the greens then chop the remaining parts into small pieces.

5. Now stack them on top of each other and then roll them into cigar shaped bundles. Now cut the greens into 1-2 inch wide pieces.

6. Mix the stems and the greens with salt and sugar and then add them to the pot, before you toss well to coat with the oil mixture.

7. Press the manual button then set the time to 20 minutes then use the quick release method to release pressure once the time lapses.

Nutritional Information Per Serving: Calories 122.5, Fat 7.4 g, Carbs 11.9 g, Protein 4.1g

63.   Spaghetti Squash with Sage Garlic Sauce

Serves: 4

Ingredients

⅛ teaspoon nutmeg

1 teaspoon salt

2 tablespoons olive oil

3-5 cloves garlic, sliced

1 small bunch fresh sage

1 cup water

1 medium spaghetti squash

Directions

1. Prepare the squash by halving it and then scoop out and discard the seeds.

2. Add water to the instant pot and put the squash at the bottom, the halves facing up. Ensure you stack them each on top of the other if you like it.

3. Close and seal the lid in place, press manual then set the time to 3-4 minutes.

4. After the 3-4 minutes, release the pressure then add sage, olive oil and garlic to a sauté pan and cook until the safe leaves are nicely fried, making sure to stir often.

5. Sage leaves should turn dark green once crispy, so keep an eye on them to avoid possible burning of the garlic slices.

6. Once cooking is up, quick release pressure and open the lid. Using a fork, pull the squash fibers out of their shells and then plop them into the waiting sauté pan.

7. After all squashes are on the pan, turn off heat and season with nutmeg and salt.

8. To serve, swoosh the ingredients to incorporate them and top with cheese.

Nutritional Information Per Serving: Calories 88.6, Fat 4g, Carbs 13.8g, Protein 1.5g

64. Artichokes with Lemon Tarragon Sauce

Serves: 4

Ingredients

1/2 cup extra-virgin olive oil

1 stalk celery

1 tablespoon finely chopped tarragon leaves

2 cups poultry bone broth

2 small lemons

4 artichokes, 5 to 6 ounces each

1/4 teaspoon

Directions

1. Prepare the artichokes by rimming the stems to get one-inch pieces.

2. Now cut off 1-inch of the petals from each end of the vegetable and then discard the petal tips and the stems too.

3. Zest the lemon and set aside. Then cut four thin sliced from the middle of the fruit, and discard the seeds.

4. Put the lemon slices in the pressure cooker and top each of the slice with the trimmed artichokes, the stem side facing up. Now pour the broth around the ingredients.

5. Close and seal the lid, press manual then set the timer to 20 minutes. After the cooking is completed, quick release the pressure.

6. Meanwhile, start preparing the dipping sauce. To do so, chop the tarragon and then trim both ends of celery stalk. Chop the celery into smaller pieces.

7. Then peel the lemon that remained and cut the white pith away using a paring knife. Coarsely chop the lemon and discard the seeds.

8. At this point, put the lemon fruit, lemon zest, olive oil, chopped celery, tarragon and salt in a food processor or blender and puree to obtain thick and creamy sauce.

9. Serve the artichoke with the dipping sauce. Also eat the soup that remains in the pressure cooker.

Nutritional Information Per Serving: Calories 226, Fat 24.1g, Carbs 7.8g, Protein 7.2g

65.   Brussels sprouts In the Instant Pot

Serves 4

Ingredients

1/4 cup Pine nuts

Salt & pepper

Olive oil

1 lb. Brussels sprouts

Directions

1. Put a trivet in an instant pot and the steamer basket on top.

2. Then pour a cup of water and add the Brussels sprouts on the basket.

3. Close and seal the lid then press manual and set the timer to 3 minutes.

4. As soon as the beep sounds, do a quick release and open the lid.

5. Season the veggies with olive oil, pepper, salt and garnish with the pine nuts if you like.

Nutritional Information Per Serving: Calories: 206, Fat: 16.1g, Carbs: 4.7g, Protein: 3.2g

66.   Steamed and Fried Artichoke Blooms

Serves 4

Ingredients

1-2 cups Olive Oil for frying

3 garlic cloves, squashed

1 tablespoon pepper corns, whole

2 lemons, 1 juiced and 1 sliced

6 artichokes, long and narrow

Directions

1. Add 2 cups of water, garlic, lemon slices, peppercorns and lemon juice to Instant pot.

2. Remove tough outer leaves from artichokes, peel the stems and discard unwanted parts off. Tease the leaves open and collect the hairy "choke" from each artichoke. Place into the Instant Pot head down.

3. Shake the artichokes to remove pepper-corns. Place the steamer basket into the Instant Pot. In case the stems are tall, simply fold them down.

4. Lock the lid, press manual then set the timer to 5 minutes. Quick release pressure, shake the artichokes and transfer into a strainer.

5. Allow them to dry for 5 minutes. Meanwhile, heat olive oil in a high-edged pan.

6. Open the artichokes, and smash them down into the oil. Fry for 3-4 minutes or until the edges become brown.

7. Transfer them to a folded towel to absorb extra oil. Serve with tart yoghurt sauce.

Nutritional Information Per Serving: Calories 116, Carbs 5.6 g, Protein 1.7 g, Fat 21.1 g

67.   Spiced Potato and Cauliflower

Serves: 4-6

Ingredients

1/2 teaspoon Garam Masala

1 teaspoon Roasted Cumin Powder

1-2 teaspoon Coriander Powder

1/4-1/2 teaspoon cayenne

1/2 teaspoon Turmeric Powder

1 teaspoon salt

1 medium tomato, chopped

1 teaspoon ginger, finely chopped

1 teaspoon garlic, finely chopped

2 cups cauliflower florets

1 cup Yukon gold potatoes, sliced

2-4 green chilies or 2 jalapeños

1/2 cup onion, sliced

1 teaspoon cumin seeds

1 tablespoon olive oil or ghee

2 tablespoons chopped cilantro

Directions

1. Add cumin seeds in an instant pot then press on the sauté function and allow them to sizzle.

2. Then add the red potatoes, green chiles and onions. Cook these ingredients for a minute or so.

3. Then add in chopped garlic and sauté for about 1 minute more. Add in salt and chopped tomatoes and sauté for 2 more minutes.

4. Now add in cauliflower florets and stir gently. Cancel the sauté function and set the instant pot to manual.

5. Cook the dish for up to a minute based on the size of potatoes and the cauliflower florets.

6. Open the lid and naturally release pressure. In case you find any liquid at the bottom, sauté for a few more minutes.

7. Garnish the meal with cilantro if you like.

Nutritional Information Per Serving: Calories 123, Fat 10.9g, Carbs 4.4g, Protein 1.5g

68. Pork-Stuffed Calabacita Squash

Serves: 6

Ingredients

6 calabacita squash, seeds removed

1/4 cup fresh chopped cilantro

14.5 ounces canned diced tomatoes

1 tablespoon butter, ghee, or coconut oil

1 1/2 teaspoons fine sea salt, divided

1 tablespoon garlic powder, divided

1 tablespoon ground cumin, divided

1 tablespoon chili powder, divided

1 pork tenderloin

For the chipotle cream sauce

1 1/2 teaspoons chipotle or chili powder

3 tablespoons fresh lime juice

1/3 cup canola-oil free mayo

Directions

1. Dust the tenderloin with half of the chili powder, sea salt, garlic and cumin.

2. Press the sauté button and then add butter to the cooking pain. Once melted, add the seasoned meat and brown each side for 3 to 4 minutes.

3. Press on the cancel button and cover the meat with water, and seal the lid. Now press on the Meat/Stew function and wait for the instant pot to reach pressure.

4. Once cooking is done, allow the cooker to naturally depressurize for about 90 minutes or so.

5. Open the lid and move the meat to a large mixing bowl and now shred into pieces. Add most of the spices along with canned tomatoes, and then stir to combine.

6. Then layer the de-seeded squash into a rimmed baking sheet or a large casserole, the cut side facing up.

7. At this point, stuff the pork and bake it at 350 degrees F, until cooked through, or for 45 minutes.

8. Meanwhile, as the squash bakes, start making the sauce. Just mix all the sauce ingredients and blend them together until smooth.

9. Once fully cooked, pour the sauce over the top and serve. You can garnish with cilantro if you like.

Nutritional Information Per Serving: Calories 116, Fat 12g, Carbs 11g, Protein 23g

69.   White Beet and Garlic Sauté

Serves 4-6

Ingredients

2 lemon wedge, squeezed

4 cloves garlic, minced

2 tablespoon olive oil

2 teaspoon salt

Water to cover

6 whole white beets

Directions

1. Wash the beets greens, strain and put aside. Then put white beets into Instant Pot. Add sufficient water to cover them and some salt.

2. Seal the Instant Pot, press on manual then set the time to 10-15 minutes. After the time lapses, quick release pressure, open the cooker and add the beet greens. Push them into the hot water to wilt.

3. Seal the lid and allow the beet greens to cook in residue heat for 5 minutes. Strain out the white beets and greens.

4. Then peel the beets, and chop into pieces. Meanwhile, preheat a sauté pan then heat oil in it.

5. Once hot, add the beets and sear for 3 minutes without stirring. Then add beet greens and garlic then cook until stems are tender.

6. Transfer the side dish to a serving plate, then drizzle with fresh lemon to serve.

Nutritional Information Per Serving: Calories 124, Fat 4.9, Carbs 5.4g, Protein 1.5g

70.   Peperonata Sauce or Side Dish

Serves 4

Ingredients

Salt and pepper

Olive oil, fresh and unfiltered

1 bunch of Basil or Parsley

2 Garlic cloves

1 red onion, sliced into thin strips

2 medium ripe tomatoes

1 green pepper, thinly sliced

2 yellow peppers, thinly sliced

2 red peppers, sliced into thin strips

Directions

1. Slice the peppers, then and chop rinse the tomatoes.

2. Heat olive oil into Instant Pot then add onions, peppers and garlic clove. Allow to brown for 5 minutes, without stirring.

3. Add in salt, pepper and tomato puree. Mix together and lock the lid of Instant Pot.

4. Press on manual then set the timer to 5-6 minutes. Then once the time lapses, quick release pressure, open the lid and take out the garlic wrapper.

5. Using tongs, remove the peppers then put them into a serving bowl. Reserve the liquid for pasta or risotto sauce.

6. To serve, add a raw pressed garlic clove, fresh swirl of olive oil and chopped basil. Mix well.

Nutritional Information Per Serving: Calories 188, Fat 18.4 g, Carbs 5.2 g Protein 2.8 g

71. Stir-Fried Broccoli

Serves 4

Ingredients

6 tablespoons chicken or vegetable stock

1 bunch broccoli stems trimmed, cut into flowerets

1 slice of ginger, fresh and peeled

1 large clove garlic, crushed and peeled

2 tablespoons olive oil

2 tablespoons Keto friendly sauce

Salt

Directions

1. In the Instant Pot, heat oil until it's very hot. Then add in ginger and garlic and stir fry to obtain a golden color.

2. Now add broccoli and stir fry until bright green, then sprinkle with salt. Transfer the mixture into the steamer basket of your cooker.

3. Then pour the sauce and stock into the bottom of the cooker, and lower the basket in.

4. Close and secure the lid, press manual then set the timer to 2 minutes. Use the quick release method to release pressure after the 2 minutes then remove the steamer basket.

5. Serve.

Nutritional Information Per Serving: Calories 156, Fat 12.4g, Carbs 1.9g, Protein, 6.1g, Fiber 3.9g

72. Tomato Spinach Quiche

Serves 6

Ingredients

1/4 cup Parmesan cheese, shredded

4 tomato slices

3 large green onions, sliced

1 cup seeded tomato, diced

3 cups fresh baby spinach, roughly chopped

1/4 teaspoon black pepper, fresh ground

1/2 teaspoon salt

1/2 cup milk

12 large eggs

Directions

1. In the bottom of the cooker, set the trivet and then add in 1 ½ cups of water.

2. Whisk together pepper, salt, milk and eggs in a large bowl. Then add in the spinach, green onions and tomato to a 1 ½ quart-baking dish and combine well.

3. Now pour the egg mixture over your veggies and stir to mix. Now spread the sliced tomatoes on the mixture and sprinkle parmesan cheese.

4. Position the dish on the trivet using a sling, then close and lock the lid. Press on manual then set the time to 20 minutes.

5. As soon as the timer beeps, turn it off and let the pressure to release naturally. After 10 minutes, quick release any remaining pressure.

6. Open the lid, lift off the dish and broil if desired until it's lightly browned; uncovered. Use a paper towel to soak any liquid that forms on top of the quiche.

Nutritional Information Per Serving: Calories 214, Carbs 12g, Fat 16g, Protein 20g

73.   Instant Pot Steamed Artichokes

Serves: 4

Ingredients

1 cup water

4 lemon wedges

4 whole artichokes, medium-sized

Directions

1. Rinse the artichokes, and then trim off the steam and top thirds using a sharp kitchen knife. Pick a lemon wedge and rub the cut top of the zucchini to prevent browning.

2. Put a steamer basket or steam rack in an Instant Pot then position the artichokes on top.

3. Pour in about 1 cup of water and then close and secure the lid.

4. Set the Instant Pot to manual and the timer for 20 minutes. In case the artichokes are large, adjust cooking time by 5 minutes.

5. Once the zucchini is cooked, turn off the Instant Pot then allow it to naturally release pressure for 10 minutes. Then quick release remaining steam by opening the valve.

5. Remove the artichokes using tongs then serve warm with desired sauce.

Nutritional Information Per Serving: Calories 71, Proteins 5.3g, Fat 0.3g, Carbs 11g

74. Instant Pot Asparagus Canes

Serves 4

Ingredients

8 ounce Prosciutto, thinly sliced

1 lb. thick Asparagus

Directions

1. Heat 1-2 cups of water in an Instant Pot (you can use any function). Wrap the asparagus spears in sliced prosciutto.

2. Put remaining unwrapped pears in one layer along the bottom of Instant Pot's steamer basket. They prevent prosciutto from sticking.

3. Now lay the wrapped asparagus in one layer. Put the basket into the Instant Pot and seal the lid. Press manual then set the time to 2-3 minutes then let it cook.

4. Then quick release and open the pot. Remove the steamer basket and transfer the prosciutto-wrapped asparagus on a serving platter.

5. Serve immediately.

Nutritional Information Per Serving: Calories 116, Carbs 8.3g, Protein 8.7g, Fat 11.1g

75.Pressure Cooker Mashed Turnips

Serves 4

Ingredients

1/2 cup beef or chicken broth

1/4 cup sour cream, dairy free

1 small onion, peeled and diced

Black pepper, freshly ground

4 medium turnips, peeled and diced

Salt

Directions

1. Into an Instant Pot, add onion, turnip and broth. Seal the lid, choose the manual option then set the time to 5 minutes and let it cook. Turn off the cooker and naturally pressure release for 10 minutes.

2. Using a slotted spoon, put the turnips onto a serving bowl. Using an immersion blender or handheld mixer, puree the turnips. Add a little broth if required.

3. Now stir in sour cream, and adjust salt and pepper accordingly.

Nutritional Information Per Serving: 25 Calories, Fat 2g, Carbs 16.4g, Protein 8.4g

76.   Pressure Cooker Beet & Caper Salad

Serves: 4 – 6

Ingredients

2 tablespoons white balsamic vinegar

4 medium beets

Dressing:

2 tablespoons capers

1 tablespoons olive oil, extra virgin

1 pinch black pepper

½ teaspoon salt

1 large garlic clove

Parsley stems removed

Directions

1. Add a cup of water and insert a steamer basket into Instant Pot.

2, Snip the beets, clean and put them into steamer basket. Lock the lid, choose manual, then set the time to 20-25. Let them cook.

3. Meanwhile, chop parsley and garlic together to make a dressing. Put into a small jar then add in capers, olive oil, salt and pepper. Close tightly and shake to incorporate.

4. Then quick release pressure and check if beets are done using a fork. If not, cook for 5 more minutes and then quick release pressure.

5. Transfer the steamer basket to the sink, and run cold water to cool the beets. Use a dull knife to brush the skins off. Slice the beets.

6. Then arrange on a serving dish and sprinkle with coconut sugar. Shake the dressing and pour into the beets. Serve.

Nutritional Information Per Serving: Calories 99, Carbs 11g, Protein 1.7g, Fat 9.5g

Perfectly Roasted Garlic

77. Serves 4

Ingredients

1 cup water

Drizzle of olive oil, extra virgin

6 large garlic bulbs

Directions

1. Add water to an Instant pot then put a steamer basket into the instant pot. Set aside.

2. Slice off the top quarter of garlic bulbs, then put them into the steamer basket.

3. Lock the lid, press on manual then set the time to 5-6 minutes. Then naturally release pressure for around 10 minutes. Use the valve to remove any remaining pressure.

4. Remove the garlic bulbs from steamer basket using tongs. Transfer into a heat-safe bowl.

5. Using olive oil, drizzle in all nooks and crannies. Then broil until golden and caramelized, say for about 5 minutes. Serve.

Nutritional Information Per Serving: Calories 46, Fat 12.4g, Carbs 1.9g net, Protein 0.1g

Eggplant & Olive Spread

Serves: 4-6

Ingredients

¼ cup black olives, pitted

1 tablespoons tahini

¼ cup of juice

½ cup water

1 teaspoon salt

3-4 garlic cloves, skin on

2 pounds eggplant

4 tablespoons olive oil

Fresh olive oil, extra virgin

Few sprigs of fresh thyme

Directions

1. Peel the eggplant and then slice chunks sufficient to cover the bottom of Instant Pot. Chop the rest finely.

2. Press sauté button, add olive oil then place the big chunks of eggplant to caramelize for 5 minutes. Then add in garlic with skin on.

3. Now flip the eggplant, and add the uncooked eggplant, salt and water. Lock the lid, press manual then set the cook time to 3 minutes.

4. Then quick release pressure, open the lid and discard the brown liquid.

5. Remove the garlic, peel out the skin. Now add in lemon juice, tahini, black olives, cooked and uncooked garlic.

5. Transfer into an immersion blender and puree until smooth. Then pour into a serving bowl and top with fresh olive oil, black olives and fresh thyme.

Nutritional Information Per Serving: Calories 123, Fat 8.9g, Carbs 1.4g, Protein 1.5g

Spicy Cauliflower Citrus Salad

Serves 4

Ingredients

2 Seedless Oranges, peeled and thinly sliced

1 pound Broccoli

1 Small Romanesco Cauliflower, florets divided

1 Small Cauliflower, florets divided

For the Vinaigrette

Pepper

Salt

4 tablespoons olive oil, extra virgin

1 tablespoon capers conserved in salt and un-rinsed

1 hot pepper, sliced or chopped

4 anchovies

1 orange, zested and squeezed

Directions

1. Add salt, pepper, olive oil, capers, hot pepper, anchovies and orange zest and juice into a vinaigrette container. Shake and set aside.

2. Peel the oranges then slice thinly cross-wise. Discard the seeds.

3. Add a cup of water into Instant Pot and put steamer basket inside.

4. Lock the lid, press manual then set the cook time to 6 minutes. Quick release pressure and move the florets into serving platter.

5. Interleave with orange slices, shake the vinaigrette and to pour on top.

Nutritional Information Per Serving: Calories 177, Fat 7.3g, Carbs 2.8g, Protein 2.2g

78. Butternut Squash Pasta

Serves: 6

Ingredients

3 cups fresh spinach, rough chopped

Salt and pepper, to taste

3.5 cups homemade bone broth

1 pound <u>penne pasta</u> (low carb)

½ medium butternut squash, 1 inch pieces

1 tablespoon bacon grease

1 tablespoon butter

2 cloves of garlic, chopped

1 small onion, chopped

2 tablespoons olive oil

6 slices bacon, chopped

Freshly grated Parmesan cheese, optional

Directions

1. Press Browning or Sauté function on your Instant Pot and allow to heat.

2. To the cooking pot, add bacon grease and sauté until crisp. Then remove the bacon from cooking pot and drain it. Reserve the cooking grease.

3. Now add in oil along with the onions and sauté until the onions are cooked through.

4. Then add in garlic, sauté for a minute and follow with pepper, salt, butter, pasta, bacon grease, bacon and the squashes.

5. Lock the lid in place and set the timer for 4 minutes. Cook until beep sounds then quick release pressure.

6. Carefully open the lid and mix in spinach to the cooking pot.

7. Serve with cheese if you like.

Nutritional Information Per Serving: Calories 151, Fat 12.4g, Carbs 6.2g, Protein 5.4g

79.   Red Cabbage Salad

Serves 4

Ingredients

Salt and pepper, to taste

1/2 teaspoon coconut sugar

1-2 teaspoons red wine vinegar

1 tablespoon olive or coconut oil

1/4 cup onion, chopped

2 cups red cabbage, shredded

Directions

1. In a steamer basket, place red cabbage and lower it into the instant pot.

2. Seal the lid and press manual then set the cook time to 1-2 minutes. Then quick release pressure.

3. Remove the steamer and cool it by running cold water over the red cabbage.

4. Then move the cabbage into another bowl and add in the other ingredients.

5. Now toss the contents and serve. If desired, you can add more vinegar and oil to taste.

Nutritional Information Per Serving: Calories 131, Carbs 5g, Fat 3g, Proteins 3g

80. Instant Pot Butternut Apple Mash

Serves 4

Ingredients

¼ teaspoon salt

¼ teaspoon cinnamon

⅛ teaspoon ginger

2 tablespoon coconut oil, butter or ghee

1 onion, quartered and sliced

2 apples, cored and sliced

1 butternut squash, cut into 2 inch pieces

1 cup water

Directions

1. Add a cup of water into an insert pot and insert a steamer basket. Then add in the onion, apples and squash. and mix well Season the mixture with salt.

2. Seal the lid, press manual then set the cook time to 8 minutes. Once cooked, quick release and pour the mixture into a bowl.

3. Now add brown butter, cinnamon and ginger. Fold the mixture to mash it then season with salt and pepper.

4. Serve and enjoy.

Nutritional Information Per Serving: Calories 133, Fat 6g, Carbs 18g, Protein 1.3g

81. Zucchini and Tomato Mélange

Serves 4

Ingredients

1 bunch of basil

Swirls of fresh olive oil

1-2 garlic cloves, finely minced

1 teaspoon salt

1 cup tomato puree

1 pound cherry tomatoes

6 medium zucchini, roughly chopped

1 tablespoon vegetable oil

2 medium onions, roughly chopped

Directions

1. Start by slicing the onion.

2. Switch the instant pot on, then press the sauté function. Add in oil and onion to cook for 5 minutes.

3. Chop the zucchini.

4. Once the onion becomes translucent, add in zucchini, cherry tomatoes, puree and pinch of salt.

5. Lock the lid, press the manual function and then cook for 5 minutes. Then quick release pressure and mix in the garlic.

6. Using a slotted spoon, strain out the veggies and serve with fresh basil leaves and olive oil.

7. Refrigerate the cooking liquid for use as chilled soup of base stock to make risotto.

Nutritional Information Per Serving: Calories 80.3, Carbs 2.7g, Protein 1.7g, Fat 3.1g

Chapter 6: Soups and Stews

82.   Keto Instant-Pot Soup Low-Carb

Serves 6

Ingredients

4 dashes hot pepper sauce

1 tablespoon Dijon mustard

6 slices cooked turkey bacon, diced

1 cup half-and-half

2 cups shredded Cheddar cheese

1 (32 fluid ounce) container chicken stock

Salt, to taste

Ground black pepper

1 green bell pepper, chopped

1 head cauliflower, coarsely chopped

1 tablespoon onion powder

2 cloves garlic, minced

1 large yellow onion, diced

1 tablespoon olive oil

Directions

1. Press on the sauté function on the instant pot then add in garlic and onion. Cook the mixture for around 3 minutes, or until browned.

2. Then add in onion powder, green bell pepper, cauliflower, salt and pepper. Pour in the stock and secure the lid.

3. Press on the soup button and set cook time to 15 minutes. Once done, quick release and wait for 5 minutes.

4. Then unlock the lid and add in hot sauce, Dijon, turkey bacon, half-and-half and cheddar cheese.

5. Press on the sauté function and now cook for around 5 minutes, or until bubbly. Serve.

Nutritional Information Per Serving: Calories 347 kcal, Fat 25.6g Carbs: 13.4g, Protein 17.7g

83. Instant Pot Chicken Soup with Kale

Servings: 4

Ingredients

1/2 teaspoon fish sauce

1 large handful kale, chopped

1 lb. cooked chicken breast, shredded

4 cups chicken broth

1/4 teaspoon dried oregano

1/2 teaspoon dried thyme

1/2 teaspoon black pepper

1 teaspoon salt

2 bay leaves

4 stalks celery, cut into bite-sized chunks

3 peeled carrots, cut into small chunks

1 medium onion, chopped

2 tablespoon butter or olive oil

Directions

1. On sauté settings, melt butter and then cook the onion until tender or for about 5 minutes or so.

2. Then add in oregano, thyme, salt, pepper, celery, carrots and the bay leaves.

3. Sauté the ingredients for 1 minute or until aromatic, then add in water and chicken broth to get up to 6-cup watermark.

4. Seal the lid then cancel the sauté function, and press on the soup function. Adjust the cook time to 4 minutes.

5. Let cook and then natural release the steam for around 15 minutes, until fully depressurized. Open the lid and add in kale and chicken.

6. Let the soup set for a minute and until the kale turns bright green. At this point, stir in the sauce along with seasonings: salt and pepper.

7. In case you use raw chicken rather than cooked, cut it into bite-sizes then brown so as the onions are tender. Then add in other ingredients.

Nutritional Information Per Serving: Calories 261, Fat 11.3g, Carbs 2.1g, Protein 35g

84.   Keto Cauliflower Soup in Instant Pot

Serves 4-6

Ingredients

6 ounce of sour cream

10 ounce of chicken broth

Fresh thyme

2 teaspoon of butter, salted

1 med. onion

5 roasted garlic cloves

1 head of cauliflower

Ground pepper

Directions

1. Roast 5 garlic cloves onto a foil in your oven for about 5 to 8 minutes. The aim is to make the outside somehow brown.

2. Meanwhile, cut the onions into quarters and then put the cauliflower, butter thyme, chicken broth and quartered onion in the cooking pot.

3. Remove the garlic from the oven and add it into the Instant pot. Set it to manual mode and set the timer for 9 minutes.

4. As soon as the timer is off, quick release and then open the lid. Add in the sour cream and puree to make soup with an immersion blender.

5. Then pour into a bowl and season with some pepper.

Nutritional Information Per Serving: Calories 79, Carbs 11g, Protein 5g, Fat 2g

85. Chicken and Wild Rice Soup Recipe

Serves 6

Ingredients

1 teaspoon pepper

1 teaspoon salt

½ teaspoon Italian seasoning

1 teaspoon minced garlic

1 teaspoon poultry seasoning

1 tablespoon parsley

¼ teaspoon rosemary

1 box Uncle Ben's quick cooking wild rice

48 ounce chicken broth

3 chicken breast, diced into cubes

1 tablespoon olive oil

1 cup carrots, diced

1 cup celery, diced

1 cup onion, diced

Directions

1. Press the sauté button then add a tablespoon of oil, celery, carrots and onions.

2. Cook the ingredients until cooked through, or for around 5 minutes. Then add in 1/3 cup of chicken broth while scrapping the bottom of the pan.

3. Follow with the diced chicken, seasons, 3 and ½ cups chicken broth and wild rice.

4. Close the lid and set cook time to 6 minutes. Wait for a few minutes for the instant pot to come into pressure.

5. Once cooking is done, natural release for about 7 minutes then quick release. You may need to place a towel on the steam release for soup not to spew out of it.

6. At this point, carefully open the lid and shred the diced chicken chunks using a fork.

7. Press the sauté button and add chicken stock into the instant pot and cook until you get your preferred consistency.

8. Let the soup boil for some time then turn off the pressure cooker.

Nutritional Information Per Serving: Calories 286, Fat 20g, Carbs 13g, Protein 23g

86.   Chicken & Smoked Sausage Stew

Serves: 6

Ingredients:

1 bay leaf

1/4 teaspoon cayenne

1/4 teaspoon black pepper

1/2 teaspoon red chili flakes, crushed

1/2 teaspoon smoked paprika

1 teaspoon thyme

1 teaspoon salt

6 cloves garlic

1/4 cup parsley

2 cups bone broth or water

2 large carrots

3 bell peppers

2 stalks celery

1 medium white onion

6 cups tomatoes, chopped

1 tablespoon coconut oil

1 pound Andouille pork sausage

1 pound boneless, skinless chicken thighs

Hot sauce, optional:

Directions:

1. Into the bottom of Instant Pot, heat coconut oil on sauté setting. Then add in sausage and chicken to instant pot and cook until cooked through.

2. Meanwhile, slice the onions, chop the celery and carrots and dice the bell peppers. Now remove the meat from the pressure cooker and set it aside.

3. Sauté the veggies as you stir regularly. Then mince garlic and add into the cooking veggies. Follow with chopped tomatoes and broth. On sauté setting, allow the mixture to simmer.

4. Once the sausage and chicken have cooled down, slice into bite-size chunks and return them to the pot. Add the spices.

5. Then mince the parsley, add it into the meat mixture and stir. Lock the lid in place and set the Instant Pot to Soup option, and cook for about 5-10 minutes.

6. Once ready, serve the chicken with hot sauce.

Nutritional Information Per Serving: Calories 237, Fat 12.35g, Carbs 10g, Protein 29.4g

87.   Keto Bacon Cheeseburger Soup

Serves: 6

Ingredients

1 cup shredded sharp cheddar cheese

4 ounces cream cheese

4 cups beef or chicken broth

4 cups cauliflower, chopped

2 stalks celery, diced

2 large carrots, diced

1 large onion, diced

1½ pounds hamburger

6 ounce bacon, chopped

Sea salt to taste

Directions

1. Press the sauté button on the instant pot and brown the bacon for a few seconds.

2. Brown the ground beef until it is cooked through then remove from the cooking pot.

3. Add the veggies and sauté for a couple of minutes or until soft. You can add in coconut oil if using lean meat.

4. Pour in broth and lock the lid. Cook for 7 minutes and then quick release the steam.

5. At this point, puree the vegetables in the cooking pot using an immersion blender.

6. Then stir in the cheeses and blend to incorporate. Also stir in the hamburger and bacon back in and allow to sit for a few minutes to warm up.

7. Serve and enjoy.

Nutritional Information Per Serving: Calories 330, Fat 17g, Protein 21g, Carbs 6g

88. Instant Pot Broccoli Cheese Soup

Servings: 4

Ingredients

2 cups almond milk

2 teaspoon seasoned salt

2 teaspoon garlic powder

1 cup water

4 cup chicken broth

5 cups shredded mixed cheese

1-2 medium carrots chopped

28 ounce frozen broccoli florets

Directions

1. Mix together defrosted broccoli, garlic powder, water, chicken broth, cheese, carrots and seasoned salt in the pressure cooker.

2. Press on the soup button and set cooking time to 5 minutes. Let the soup cook until it reduces in half.

3. Then quick release and stir in almond milk. Garnish the soup with spinach and sour cream.

Nutritional Information Per Serving: Calories 120, Protein 10.4g, Fat 10.9g, Carbs 12.6g

89. Butternut Squash Soup

Serves: 5

Ingredients

1/2 cup unsweetened, plain almond milk

3 1/2 cups low-sodium vegetable broth

2 frozen packs butternut squash, pre-cubed

¼ teaspoon pepper

¾ teaspoons salt

2 cloves garlic, minced

½ large white onion, chopped

½ tablespoon extra-virgin olive oil

Garnish ideas

Black pepper, freshly ground

Fresh chives

Cashew crème

Directions

1. Add garlic, onions, oil, salt and pepper to the Instant Pot then press on the sauté function.

2. Cook until fragrant and the onions become translucent and tender or for 3 to 5 minutes. Stir from time to time to ensure regular cooking.

3. Now add in butternut squash along with the broth. Close the lid and press on the soup setting and set the timer at 7 minutes.

4. Once cooking is over, natural release pressure and then open the cover. Add in plant milk and puree into the cooking pot using an immersion blender until smooth and creamy.

5. Serve the soup with garnishes such as chives, cashew cream and black pepper. You can leave it under keep warm setting is not serving immediately.

Nutritional Information Per Serving: Calories 132, Fat 2.2g, Carbs 9.4g, Protein 1.9g

90. Pressure Cooker Tomato Soup

Serves 6

Ingredients

1 quart coconut or almond milk

1/3 cup coconut or almond flour

1/2 cup butter

1/2 teaspoon pepper flakes

1/4 teaspoon pepper

1/4 teaspoon dried basil

1 each bay leaf

1 teaspoon salt

1 tablespoon white sugar

2 teaspoon beef bouillon

2 lb. fresh tomatoes

Sour cream, yoghurt or cheese for garnish

Directions

1. In an Instant Pot, put basil, bay leaf, pepper flakes, pepper, salt, coconut sugar, bouillon and tomatoes then mix well.

2. Press the soup button and cook for 30 minutes.

3. Once done, put the tomato mixture through a strainer or food mill to remove the bay leaf and tomato skins. If desired, freeze or refrigerate the tomato mixture for later use.

3. Then, melt butter into a large sauce pan then whisk in coconut or almond floor. Cook the mixture for 1 minute.

4. At this point, add in coconut milk and stir to thicken the soup. Stir in the tomato mixture, and then heat through. If desired, add yoghurt, dairy-free cheese or sour cream.

Nutritional Information Per Serving: Calories 273.5, Fat 14.5g, Carbs 5g, Protein 20.6g

91. Buffalo Chicken Soup

Serves 4

Ingredients

2 cups heavy cream

4 cups cheddar cheese, shredded

2/3 cup hot sauce

4 tablespoons ghee or butter

2 tablespoon ranch dressing mix

2 clove garlic, chopped

1/8 cup diced onion

1 cup diced celery

6 cups chicken bone-broth

4 boneless skinless chicken breasts

Directions

1. Mix all the ingredients in an Instant Pot apart from cream and cheese.

2. Without locking the lid, cook for 10 minutes (you can use the sauté function or manual function).

3. Gently remove the chicken, shred it using two forks and return into the soup.

4. Add in dairy free heavy cream and Paleo cheese. Stir to incorporate.

Nutritional Information Per Serving: Calories 285.3, Carbs 17.6g, Fat 17.6g, Protein 24g

92.   Italian Wedding Soup

Serves 4-6

Ingredients

1 tablespoon of lard, avocado oil or ghee

1/2 teaspoon sea salt

1/2 teaspoon of garlic powder

1 cup spinach, chopped

1 cup carrots, diced

1 onion, diced

1/2 teaspoon onion powder

64 ounces broth

Pepper to taste

For the Meatballs

1 teaspoon garlic powder

Pinch sea salt

1 tablespoon 100% maple syrup

2 tablespoons coconut aminos

3 tablespoons coconut milk

3 tablespoons water chestnut flour

1 pound organic turkey, ground

1 tablespoon nutritional yeast, optional

Directions

1. Begin by preheating the oven to 350 degree F.

2. Then, combine meatball ingredients in a bowl. Make 1-2 inch meatballs and put them onto a baking sheet lined with parchment.

3. Bake the meatballs for 10-12 minutes in the oven then set aside.

4. Now sauté onion with cooking fat inside the instant pot until it becomes translucent and slightly brown.

5. Then add in carrots, meatballs, broth and seasonings. If desired, add couscous too but reserve the spinach.

6. Secure the lid, set the soup function and cook for 10 minutes. Then quick release pressure, open the lid and stir in chopped spinach.

7. Stir until spinach wilts. To thicken the soup, add tapioca starch and serve.

Nutritional Information Per Serving: Calories 260, Fat 6g, Carbs 16g, Protein 4g

93.   Instant Pot Pumpkin Soup

Serves: 6

Ingredients:

250 ml coconut milk

½ apple, peeled, cored and grated

2 bay leaves

Cracked black pepper

375 ml chicken stock

Curry powder

½ brown onion, chopped

½ red potato or radishes, diced

½ butternut pumpkin, chunks

½ tablespoon butter

Directions

1. In an Instant Pot, melt butter and then add in onion, potato, pumpkin chunks and some curry powder.

2. Cook over low heat to lightly brown the onion as you stir regularly.

3. Add the chicken stock followed by bay leaves and black pepper.

4. Lock the lid, press manual and set the cook time to 5 minutes.

5. Once done, release the pressure and then stir in the grated apples. Cook for 10 minutes when uncovered, as you stir.

6. Take out the bay leaves and process the soup in a blender. Now add some milk in to help achieve desired creamy or smooth consistency.

7. If you like it, serve with a few croutons, preferably in warmed bowls.

Nutritional Information Per Serving: Calories 146, Fat 5g, Carbs 11g, Protein 1.8g

94. Creamed Fennel and Cauliflower Soup

Serves: 4

Ingredients:

2 teaspoons salt

3 cups bone or vegetable broth

1 cup coconut milk

1 pound cauliflower florets

1 extra-large fennel bulbs, stalks and fronds removed

3 cloves garlic

1 white onion

1 tablespoon coconut oil

Black pepper

Truffle oil, optional

Directions

1. Chop the fennel, mince the garlic and slice the onions. Press sauté function on the instant pot then add oil and then sauté the onion until transparent.

2. Add in chopped cauliflower florets, fennel and garlic then sauté until the edges in veggies become golden.

3. After about 5-10 minutes of cooking, pour coconut milk and broth into the pot. Add in salt and cook for 5 more minutes.

4. Quick release pressure, remove the lid and transfer the mixture into an immersion blender or standing blender. Puree until smooth.

5. To serve, scoop the hot soup into serving bowls. Drizzle with truffle oil and top with cracker pepper. Garnish with fennel frond.

Nutritional Information Per Serving: Calories 114.3, Fat 7.79g, Proteins 3.91g, Carbs 9.21g

95.   Curried Cream of Broccoli Soup

Serves 6

Ingredients

1 cup full-fat coconut milk

Black pepper, freshly-ground

4 cups bone broth or chicken stock

¼ cup peeled apple, diced

1½ pounds broccoli, chopped

Kosher salt

1 tablespoon Indian curry powder

2 medium shallots, chopped

3 medium leeks, chopped

2 tablespoons olive oil, coconut oil or ghee

Chives, garnish

Leftover Kalua Pork, crisped in a pan

Directions

1. Prepare and chop the broccoli, leeks or onions. Press the sauté button on Instant Pot, add fat and then cook the shallots, leeks, curry powder and salt.

2. Cook for 5 minutes, stirring occasionally until the curry is fragrant. Now stir in chopped broccoli and apple.

3. Follow with broth and ensure the Instant Pot isn't more than 2/3rd full. Cook the mixture (use manual function to set the cook time) for 5 minutes.

4. Then turn off the cooker and quick release the pressure. Now open the lid and transfer the ingredients into a blender. Puree to produce a green aromatic soup.

5. Add in coconut milk and season with salt and some pepper. Continue to blend as desired.

6. You can add crisped-up meat such as Kalua pork and garnish with chives. Save up to 4 days and freeze for a few months.

Nutritional Information Per Serving: 125 Calories, Fat 10g, Carbs 18g, Protein 4.0g

96.   Keto Chicken "Noodle" Soup

Serves: 4

Ingredients

⅛ teaspoon pepper, fresh ground

1 teaspoon grey sea salt

½ teaspoon dried oregano

½ teaspoon dried basil

6 cups chicken stock

¾ cup chopped green onion

1 cup diced carrots

1 cup diced celery

1 pound chicken thighs, boneless and skinless

2 tablespoons coconut oil

2 cups spiralized daikon noodles

Directions

1. Add chicken thighs and coconut oil to the bowl of Instant Pot.

2. Set sauté function for 10 minutes. Cook the chicken and then shred with a fork.

3. Then add in onions, carrots and celery and cook for 2 minutes.

4. At this point, add the other ingredients. Close the lid and press the Soup button.

5. Cook for 15 minutes then add daikon noodles once ready.

Nutritional Information Per Serving: Calories 295, Fat 10.7g, Carbs 7.2g, Protein 43.2g

97.   Instant Pot Goulash

Serves 6

Ingredients

2 teaspoons lemon juice

100 ml coconut milk or cream

2 tablespoon fresh parsley, chopped

1 - 2 teaspoons arrowroot powder

Salt and pepper

1 organic, beef stock cube, gluten free

2 teaspoon coconut oil

2 heaped tablespoon tomato paste

600 g raw tomato puree

3 tablespoons paprika

3 cloves of garlic, crushed

1 yellow pepper, thinly sliced

1 green pepper, sliced

1 red pepper, thinly sliced

1 large onion, thinly sliced

800 g - 1 kg diced beef

1 Hungarian paprika sausage, optional

Directions

1. Heat a teaspoon of oil in an Instant Pot then fry the meat in the oil (using the sauté function). Cook them in batches and brown each before adding the next.

2. Once all meat has browned, remove from pan, add a teaspoon of coconut oil and fry the peppers or onion until about to soften.

3. Then put the meat to the pan and add in crushed garlic. Stir it well and sprinkle over the meat and pepper mixture.

4. At this point, add in the raw tomato puree, tomato paste and beef stock. Stir well. Close the lid and press the meat button, and then cook for about 40 minutes.

5. Once cooked, turn off the cooker; allow natural release of pressure for 10-15 minutes. Meanwhile, prepare beetroot noodles and cauliflower rice.

6. As it cooks, remove the lid and inspect the consistency of the sauce. You can add arrowroot powder mixed with some cold water to thicken. Stir to achieve thicker consistency.

7. Add in chopped parsley but reserve some for garnish. Then season with pepper and salt. If desired, stir through coconut or sour cream, or simply pour on top of the goulash.

Nutritional Information Per Serving: Calories: 360, Fat: 27g Carbs: 17g, Protein: 21g

98.   Instant Pot Carne Guisada

Serves 4-6

Ingredients

1 tablespoon arrow root starch

½ cup tomato sauce

1 cup beef broth or chicken stock

½ teaspoon oregano

½ teaspoon chipotle powder

½ teaspoon pepper

1 teaspoon salt

1 teaspoon paprika

1 teaspoon chili powder

1 teaspoon ground cumin

1 bay leaf

1 Serrano peppers, minced

1 tablespoon minced garlic

1 onion, diced

1 pound beef stew meat

2 tablespoons avocado oil

Directions

1. Press on the sauté function then add oil into the Instant Pot. Add in beef cubes and sear the meat on all sides.

2. Once the beef cubes have browned, add in the spices, bay leaf, Serrano pepper, garlic and onion. Stir fry for around 2-3 minutes.

3. Then pour in the tomato sauce and beef broth and proceed to lock the lid. Press on Warm/Cancel and then the Meat/stew function and cook the meat for 35 minutes. As you do this, ensure the steam valve has been closed.

4. Natural release pressure for 10-15 minutes then unlock the lid. Ladle a little of the liquid in a bowl and add in potato flour. Combine and stir the thick slurry into the pot.

5. Serve the dish over tortilla or cauli-rice.

Nutritional Information Per Serving: Calories 320, Fat 6g, Protein 18g, Carbs 12g

99.   Pressure-Cooker Lamb Stew

Serves 4-5

Ingredients:

1/4-1/2 teaspoon salt

3 tablespoon broth or water

6 cloves garlic, sliced

1 bay leaf

1 sprig rosemary

1 large yellow onion

3 large carrots

1 acorn squash

2 lbs. lamb stew meat, cut into 1" cubes

Directions

1. Prepare the acorn squash: peel, seed and cube it. You can microwave for a minute before cutting it.

2. Slice the carrots, peel the onion and slice it into half-moons. Cut the veggies either bigger or smaller depending on your choice.

3. Put all the ingredients into the Instant Pot and press on the soup/stew setting then let cook for 35 minutes.

4. Quick release pressure and unlock the lid. Serve and enjoy.

Nutritional Information Per Serving: Calories 273.5, Fat 14.5g, Carbs 15g, Protein 2.6g

100. Instant Pot Beef Stew

Serves 4

Ingredients

1 tablespoon maple syrup

2 large sweet potato, peeled & cubed

1 tablespoon avocado oil or olive oil

1/2 cup beef broth/stock

1 cup red wine

2 teaspoon black pepper, ground

2 tablespoon parsley

2 tablespoon thyme

2 teaspoon rock salt

2 cloves garlic minced

1 large red onion, peeled and sliced

5 medium carrots cut into sticks

1/2 lb. bacon tips or rashers

1 lb. stewing steak or flank steak

Directions

1. On Browning settings, put a teaspoon of oil into the cooking basket of Instant Pot and warm.

2. Then pat dry the beef and season it. Sauté the meat in batches and allow each patch to brown. Set aside.

3. Now slice the bacon and then brown along with the onions. Add the beef back along with other ingredients.

4. Set the Instant Pot to high pressure and cook for about 30 minutes. Serve and enjoy.

Nutritional Information Per Serving: Calories 301, Carbs 17g, Fat 10g, Protein 31g

101. Pressure Cooker Chicken Enchilada Soup

Serves: 6

Ingredients:

1 tablespoon olive oil, extra virgin

2 cups sliced carrots

2 cups sliced celery

2 cups sweet potatoes, peeled and diced

½ cup diced yellow onions

2 cloves garlic, minced

2 tablespoons taco seasoning

1½ teaspoon sea salt

½ teaspoon black pepper

1 18-ounce jar diced tomatoes

2 cups cubed butternut squash

5 cups chicken stock

2 pounds chicken breast, boneless and skinless

2 teaspoons lime juice

Optional

Plantain chips

Lime wedges

Cilantro

Directions:

1. Press sauté button on your instant pot then add in olive oil, garlic, onion, celery, carrot, taco seasoning, salt and pepper.

2. Cook for about 5 minutes, stirring. Then stir in other ingredients.

3. Set the Instant Pot to Soup Mode and time for 5 minutes. When cooked, quick release pressure but avoid contact with the hot steam.

4. Set the chicken to a platter, shred it using two forks and then return it into the cooking pot. Stir.

5. Now pour the soup into bowls and serve with plantain chips, lime wedges and cilantro.

Nutritional Information Per Serving: Calories 373, Fat 11.8g, Carbs 14.1g, Protein 51.5g

102.   Beef Stew with Turnips and Carrots

Serves: 4

Ingredients

¼ cup fresh parsley, chopped

¼ cup coconut aminos

1 pound carrots, 1 inch pieces

1 pound turnips, 1 inch pieces

1 cup bone broth

1 cup dry red wine

1 teaspoon dried thyme

2 tablespoons cassava flour

1 medium red onion, chopped

2 tablespoons bacon grease or coconut oil

Salt

1 pound beef stew meat, 1 inch pieces

Directions

1. Start by seasoning the beef with salt.

2. Then press sauté function on the instant pot. After the instant pot becomes hot, add 1 tablespoon of fat to melt.

2. Add seasoned beef and brown on all sides for around 8 minutes. Then remove the meat from Instant Pot and set aside.

3. Add the onions and the rest of the fat into the Instant Pot and cook for 5 minutes or until soft, while stirring.

4. Stir in thyme and cassava flour and cook for 1 minute. Then whisk in wine and scrap browned bits from the bottom of cooking pot.

5. At this point, stir in coconut aminos, carrots, turnips and broth along with the reserved broth.

6. Close the lid and press on the Meat/Stew function. Cook then natural release pressure for 10 minutes.

7. Quick release, open the lid and serve the stew into bowls. Garnish with parsley.

Nutritional Information Per Serving: Calories 326, Carbs 23g, Fat 10g, Protein 29g

Conclusion

We have come to the end of the book. Thank you for reading and congratulations for reading until the end.

As far as options go, you won't be short of them when you follow a Ketogenic diet because there are just so many recipes that you can prepare. And given that you can leverage on the power of the instant pot in retaining the nutritional information in foods and the fact that the instant pot fastens cooking, you can be sure that you won't have any reason not to eat Ketogenic diet friendly recipes. I hope this book has opened your eyes to the endless possible ways through which you can prepare keto friendly meals using an instant pot. Now is your time to take action i.e. choosing any of the recipes here to follow the Ketogenic diet like a pro!

If you found the book valuable, can you recommend it to others? One way to do that is to post a review on Amazon.

Click here to leave a review for this book on Amazon!

Thank you and good luck!

50193860R00115

Made in the USA
Columbia, SC
03 February 2019